WRITIN

BY RUTH COLLINS

Published by Starry Night Publishing
Rochester, New York

Ruth Collins

"I did not choose this. This chose me." ~Laura D., Minnesota protective mother and child-safety advocate.

"I alone cannot change the world, but I can cast a stone across the waters to create many ripples." ~Unknown

"Hatred paralyzes life; love releases it. Hatred confuses life; love harmonizes it. Hatred darkens life; love illuminates it." ~Dr. Martin Luther King, Jr.

"Your story is the key that can unlock someone else's prison. Share your testimony." ~Spiritual Inspiration

"Sometimes music is the only medicine the heart and soul need." ~tinybuddha.com

"As soon as healing takes place, go out and heal somebody else." ~Maya Angelou

Ruth Collins

CONTENTS

DEDICATION

I dedicate this book to warrior-mother Donna Buiso, whose memoir *Nothing But My Voice* inspired me to sharpen my listening skills and, more importantly, to take action.

It is the year 2018. I acknowledge that I belong to a tribe of warriors that no one from outside that tribe talks about. I know their names — and they know mine. More than likely, we've never met in person but instead, online. This tribe I speak of consists of female warriors: I will refer to them as protective mothers. My tribe is female warriors denied "life, liberty, and the pursuit of happiness."

Our kinship validates our existence as we walk invisible amongst you.

You may wonder what brought us — strangers — together. Why would thousands or possibly tens of thousands of women join forces and support each other? Here is my answer: We are united in the fact that through no fault of our own, we have been left with nothing but our voices. We have been left childless, financially disabled, heartbroken, hopeless, shell-shocked, numb, and disabled with post-traumatic stress disorder and an overwhelming sense of being alone. We speak, but no one hears us. We cry, but no one wipes our tears. We scream, but our screams go unheard. We go through the motions of life, but we do so as if we are moving through quicksand.

Some well-intentioned people attempt to comfort us with assurance that everything will be just fine, but it never is. Imagine being deprived of an active role in nurturing, loving, and guiding a young child into young adulthood. Assuring us that all will be fine is a cue that you are not truly listening. How can one mourn the death of a relationship that people insist still has the opportunity to be? If I could ask these well-meaning people one thing, it would be this: Please, stop telling me that my children will "come back." Because truth be told, there is a good chance they will not. And, even if they do return, they will not be the children I once knew. I assure you, trauma has a way of changing people for life.

Let me introduce you to one of the newest members of my tribe, Donna Buiso. She, like me, through several years of family court procedures, was stripped of all parental rights. I purchased her memoir hoping to find the answer to the question that every mother denied time with her children wants to know. "Do the children ever come back? Do the children deprived of their biological mother ever come to really know her?" Donna Buiso's poignant message will be threaded throughout my memoir. In the words David P. Hayes uses to describe her book, "This is a book that requires action. Action to change and rectify a system that allows the continued unconscionable abuse of mothers. These injustices must be corrected for the sake of all emotionally abused mothers, their emotionally abused children, and for the welfare of society at large."

Donna Buiso's depiction of her life with an emotionally abusive ex-husband can be triggering for anyone who has lived this kind of hell. Psychological warfare is the only way to describe what it is like to co-parent with an abusive ex-partner. Mr. and Mrs. John Q. Public often forget that emotional, verbal, financial, and judicial abuse fall within the spectrum of domestic abuse. Imagine being court-ordered to stand back and watch your child suffer verbal, emotional, and psychological abuse by a parent who can only focus on their own needs.

Like Donna Buiso, I was stripped of my parental rights, decision-making power, and visitation. I was court-ordered to sit back and watch as my children were raised in a home environment that lacked supervision, compassion, and unconditional love. I had to endure phone calls, emails, and text messages from my teenage daughter asking, "Where is dad taking me?" and "When can I move back in with you?"

I later found out that one of her father's tactics for controlling her behavior and disempowering her voice was to threaten her with being "dropped off somewhere" because he could no longer "handle her." When she begged and pleaded to live with the protective mother who had nurtured her for the first 12 years of her life, her father would respond, "Anywhere but with your mother." Even today, as I recount these events, I go numb. I cannot fathom how any adult — and especially a parent — could be so cruel toward a child or how a judge could deny a child their mother.

Buiso ends her book with these words: "My voice is my strength. It's all I have left. I will continue to use it, not just for myself but for the children and for all of the mothers who find themselves fighting to protect their family in court."

She has spoken. And so, have thousands and thousands of other mothers throughout the United States. We warriors write incessantly to our local and national political leaders as well as to major network television studios. Our screams, our pleas, our fears seemingly fall upon deaf ears. As such, we warriors have been left with nothing but our voices. For decades now, we have proven to be beyond brave for articulating our pain. What remains to be seen is this: Are you brave enough to listen? And, just as importantly, are you motivated to answer our call to action?

Ruth Collins

ACKNOWLEDGMENTS

First and foremost, I want to acknowledge my children, the two souls brought to this Earth who taught me what the word brave truly means. My son and daughter are brave personified. Their births led me toward a path of love, light, peace, and empowerment as well as to the level of forgiveness that only a mother's unconditional love knows. My children, my love for you grows deeper and deeper each and every day.

Secondly, I want to acknowledge that this book would not be possible without the support of my present husband, my network of trauma experts, domestic abuse advocates, protective mothers, and legislative advocates, my dearest friends, and immediate family members.

Special thanks to my editor: Without her expertise, this book would not be possible. Thank you for helping me find my voice.

More importantly, thank you, my readers, for allowing my experiences to be a figurative permission slip for other protective mothers like me — and grown children like mine — to be empowered to speak their truths as well. In doing so, my hope is that, collectively, we will be using our voices for the greater good, to end the reign of terror often experienced after a divorce.

Ruth Collins

FORWARD

I am so honored to write something on behalf of this wonderful book by Ruth Collins.

Ruth and I belong to one of those clubs that no one wants to be in: mothers grieving the loss of their live children. To be separated and erased from the lives of your children is a pain beyond words. Being unable to protect them from physical, emotional, and/or sexual abuse is torture.

Those of us in this club are familiar with terms like coercive control, domestic violence by proxy, and narcissistic personality disorder. We are familiar with the injustices of "family" court. We are aware of the stories of our sisters; each one more horrific than the next. Things are not always as they seem. Good mothers do lose custody of and contact with their children. For some, the pain is overwhelming. Missing birthdays, holidays, and milestones is bad enough, but knowing that your child might be hurting and you're not able to help them is soul-crushing. Some mothers have committed suicide. Many mothers have contemplated it.

Some, like me, have lived with this hell for way too many years. For others, I'm sure it *feels* like way too many years. Trying not to fall into the pit of despair is a daily challenge. Often, things feel dark and hopeless. This is why Ruth's book is so vital.

Writings in the Sand offers hope, not necessarily the hope that our children will return to us. Sadly, as someone who not only grieves her children but now grieves her grandchildren, I know that may never happen. However, this book gives hope that we cannot only survive, but we can thrive.

Writings in the Sand reminds us to keep our faces to the sun, to focus on the beauty around us, to live our truth, and to never give in to the darkness. In that reminder there is hope. If we can overcome our pain and live a life that reflects beauty and our truth, then we can find peace amidst the pain. If we can do this, then there is hope that our children can do it too.

Ruth's book is a must-read for any mother — or father — who is, was, or will be going through the nightmare we have endured. It is also a must-read for anyone who knows someone going through this trauma.

Donna Buiso, author of *Nothing But My Voice*

PREFACE

The term childless mother may seem like an oxymoron, but for thousands and thousands of mothers across the United States, it is not. Some parents lose their children through death, as in the case of my present husband, Joseph. Sadly, he and his first wife lost their son when he reached the tender age of 13. The loss of a child is the kind of a pain I once thought unimaginable. Now, not only can I imagine their pain, I have relived a type of death in the midst of life over and over again for years. I now understand that losing a child who is still living can be very much like losing a child through death.

July 31, 2016, was my firstborn's 20th birthday. In years past, I was privileged to have the right to see Matthew in person to celebrate along with other family members. These birthday celebrations included cards, laughter, gifts, ice cream, and cake. There was a sense of togetherness and belonging as well as unconditional love and joy. Sadly, in July of 2016, I was blocked from even leaving a simple voicemail message. I did mail Matthew a birthday card, hoping to foster some form of communication, but my card went unacknowledged. Just one month prior, I was threatened with police intervention if I chose to stop by Matthew's home just to say hello.

Let me explain. In the years following our divorce, I never showed up at Matthew's father's house unannounced. Prior to our children aging out of the family court system, I had to ask permission from Matthew's father if I wanted to see my children or drop off gifts. In 2016, as my children reached the ages of 18 and almost 20, I wanted to begin our new journey free from their father's control by communicating directly with my son and daughter. I called and texted both teenagers, asking their permission to stop by with a gift. Despite their willingness to see me, my arrival to drop off personal items and gifts that June evening was reframed as me showing up unannounced. As such, Matthew warned me via private Facebook message that if I was to ever stop by their house, one of them would be forced to call the local police. I was left to assume that he had been coached to use threats of police intervention if I made any attempt to see either of my children in person because never in our almost-20-year, mother-and-son relationship were unkind words or threats ever spoken between us. Only two people in the last 10 years have threatened me with police action. Those two were grown adults. One was my former husband and the father of my children, and the other will be explained in more detail later within this book.

As for my daughter Amber, she was coerced to go "no contact" with me. All of these mind-numbing events suddenly began after my young-adult children gave me permission to drop off items for them at their father's home. The day was a Wednesday. The time was early evening after my work shift was over. The date was June 29, 2016. Amber was last at my home in a neighboring state on the 30th of May of the same year when my husband and I hosted a high school graduation celebration for her. On that day, she seemed unusually distant and riddled with anxiety. Mother's intuition told me that something was amiss, but in front of family and friends was not the time to ask Amber what was troubling her. In hindsight, I am left to believe the direction to have no contact with me had been brewing in her father's home long before those end-of-June events.

With Amber's graduation, her father could no longer control me with frivolous family court petitions. Both Matthew and Amber would leave for college that fall; their father, I can only guess, slowly unraveled emotionally as he started losing control of all three of us. His power over me was about to end. Or, so I thought.

In reality, that summer led to the deepest grief I ever knew: a new journey of extreme maternal deprivation and coercive control post-divorce judgment. It was something I never could have imagined since our divorce had been initiated and agreed to 10 years prior.

On Sunday, July 10 2016, my soon-to-be 20-year-old son, publicly announced via social media that he was opting to "go no contact" with his mother. True to his word, Matthew has maintained his "no contact" promise. Amber texted occasionally and called once when she was having car trouble. For months, my attempts to communicate with her would go without acknowledgment or response. As a protective mother, I must dig deep and realize that the trauma of domestic violence by proxy and the effects of coercive control have adversely affected both of my children. I do not take anything personally. For several years I have been deep in the throes of self-examination and reflection and have grown to understand that how people choose to treat you is not a reflection of who you are; instead, it is a reflection of the person's character and where they are in their spiritual journey. My son and daughter have been told untruths for years. Their actions do not reflect a lack of love in their own hearts but, rather, the lack of love within the hearts of those adults responsible for our family's fracture.

My faith whispers to me that you both will return to my loving arms: I pray. I hope. I wait.

Ruth Collins

Chapter 1
Protective Mothers: Lead with Love

"So take these words,
And sing out loud
'Cause everyone is forgiven now,
'Cause tonight's the night the world begins again."
~Goo Goo Dolls, "Better Days."

Not everyone can lead with love. Some people capture others' attention by their works, their status, their money, their humor, and their version of reality. But, a few do lead with love. A parent — specifically a healthy, well-intentioned parent — can lead with love, the kind of love that is authentic, nonjudgmental, kind, compassionate, and confident. Brave warrior mothers, I suggest you lead with love. Love is the beacon that will shine bright to bring our children home.

How do you know? Your children have chosen to go no contact with you. So, how do you know what to lead with?

All I can say is I just know, with a deep knowing led by an even deeper faith. Over the years, I have found a gift. Digging deep into self-awareness and reflection, I have found the reconnection to my feminine intuition. Some commonly refer to this gift as a mother's intuition.

Decades ago, I used to bury myself with being too busy. I now understand this "busyness" was a maladaptive coping mechanism. And if busyness was not enough, I added in noise — loud music, television, more music, face-to-face dialogue, email conversations, and, of course, the ever-so-famous, over-scheduled schedule. I was alive but also asleep. And by asleep, I mean creating too many day-to-day distractions to hear my intuition: my deep knowing, which I describe as my present level of understanding of life, as well as the knowledge of who I was and what my life purpose was. Intuitively, I knew I was on this Earth for a reason. I was not just here to be using up its resources and taking up space.

In March of 1995, I married my first husband, and we had our children right away. Matthew was born 16 months after his father and I were married, Amber 20 months after Matthew's birth. Unbeknownst to me, their births began my spiritual awakening. I loved Matthew with all my heart and soul. I felt my priorities shift. Everything was about mothering and being the best mother I could possibly be. I wanted so much for my son. I wanted him to have a life far better than my own. I wanted no harm to ever come his way. The world was spinning as usual, but news stories took on a whole new significance — from the Columbine school shootings to the arrest of a local YMCA swim coach and church deacon who had allegedly abused children entrusted to their care. Those headlines led me to dabble as a volunteer child-safety advocate. The year was 1996. Answers to the prevention of child abuse seemed simple: education, awareness, solution-based activism, and the simple act of caring about our nation's greatest asset: our children. The topic was heavy, I knew, but the solutions seemed relatively easy. Or so I thought.

Amber was born in 1998. Her birth and her beautiful smile soon after her birth are moments I will never forget. If Mathew's birth was the figurative opening of the door to my awakening, Amber's birth was the kick in the butt through that door. Within months, if not weeks, my mother-bear instincts set in. No one would ever, ever, ever harm a hair on the heads of my two children. It is possible that I became overly protective. But, in truth, I had insight to that tendency, and it was easily tempered by their father, who had a different worry after their births: financial concerns.

Today, I can attribute those differences between their father and me not to one parent caring more than the other but instead to how we had been raised. I came from a family where several family members had abused others, and that was something that had followed one generation into the next. Each of us had survived our family's dysfunctional relationships as best we could. Ned's family was also dysfunctional but in ways that went unnoticed during our months of dating. Ned's family was wealthy enough to afford two homes and two new-model vehicles. Yet, financial worries plagued that family and do even to this day. It is actually very sad, as I reflect on the years upon years of worry over assets. I recognize that on a primitive level, fear is fear. Fear for one's personal safety is fear. Fear of never having enough is also fear. Fear is over powering and sometimes paralyzing. I recognized this at some point in my marriage and knew I wanted to live without fear. In hindsight, to live without fear was a tall order for both Ned and me.

Ned was obsessed with his work. It seemed that he perceived every hour he was not at work as an hour that we as a family lost money. The best two examples I can think of are these: We married on a Saturday but did not honeymoon until the following Wednesday. Ned had just started his own business, and he feared the time off for our honeymoon would set us back financially. As a supportive new wife, I agreed that an abbreviated honeymoon was sufficient. Our quality time together as honeymooners was limited to Thursday, Friday, and Saturday. The second example is the births of our children. Coincidently, both of our children were born on a Wednesday, and I was discharged from the hospital on a Friday each time. Ned "gave" me, as he explained it, all of Saturday and Sunday to be helpful around the house, but due to the added stress of our growing financial needs, he chose to return to work each Monday after my return from the hospital. I felt abandoned and suddenly sensed I was more of a burden to my husband than a cherished spouse who had just given birth to his child. If I wanted to feel sorry for myself, I could have, but instead I chose to focus on the two greatest gifts ever given to me by God: Matthew and Amber. Our children became my whole world.

Ned operated his business within our home, and I took on the responsibility of home management as well as child-rearing entirely on my own. I became so conscious of protecting my husband's assets that I offered to be our own real-estate agent when Ned decided to move our family to a nearby state where we could get more house for less money. I was extremely proud that my ability to sell our first home saved our family more than $20,000. That was December of 1999. While the whole world was panicking and preparing for Y2K, I was single-handedly raising a 20-month old, a two-and-a-half year-old, and being sales agent and mover all at once. I had no time to fixate on Y2K. The love I had for my husband, our two children, and our new adventure was enough to spur me into action to provide what I thought would be a wonderful childhood for our young children.

Even now, I can truly state that every decision and every action was motivated by the love I have for Matthew and Amber. Since the moment I found out I was pregnant with Matthew, I began to think beyond myself. Prenatal visits were the catalyst. I knew then that every choice I made would affect the growth and development of my child. I do not point this out to place myself on a pedestal but instead to illustrate that a mother's life changes the day her pregnancy is confirmed. To this day, I think long and hard about every life decision that I make. I dig deep and I ask myself, "How will this choice affect Matthew and Amber?" I think that question hindered the publication of this memoir. I did not want to publish something that had the potential to harm them in any way. However, if our relationship never heals, what do I want Matthew and Amber to know? What if my silence and my eventual death leave them with a legacy of untruths? What if they never get a chance to know the truth? What if they believe I never loved them? That thought became the motivation behind this memoir.

I write because I am choosing to lead with love. I choose unconditional love for them both. I choose to forgive the choices and behaviors that hurt me. I choose love. It is that simple. Love brought them into this world, and until my last dying breath, I offer them my love. God gave them free will. As young adults navigating their personal journey, they will need to choose as well.

In December of 2016, Matthew and Amber, I penned this poem for both of you.

Forgive Him. Love Him. But, Please Don't…
Please don't go through life feeling "less than."
God makes no mistakes: Trust me, you are "more than."
In my heart, you are God's greatest gift. I assure you, you are "more than."
Forgive him. Love him.

But, please don't define your life by your material possessions.

The adage that money buys happiness is far from true. Happiness is an inside job: It begins with self-love and self-respect.

Forgive him. Love him.

But, please don't play by his rules.

No child, young or old, should be told to choose a parent;

It is possible to love, forgive, and enjoy time spent with a mother and a father.

Do not forsake the one whose heart beats in sync with yours.

Forgive him. Love him.

But, please don't live in fear of your dreams, passions, and life calling.

Some adults choose safety and financial gain over their life purpose.

To choose to live in fear is to place yourself in shackles, And then hide the key in your own coat pocket.

Free yourself. Only you have the power to free yourself from the fear of failure.

Forgive him. Love him.

But please don't choose to build a wall around your heart.

Emotional detachment from people is a sign that you are not living life.

Be vulnerable: Love, listen, respect, be joyful, and be open to new journeys.

Forgive him. Love him.

But please don't let him re-create your childhood memories.

Seek the truth.

The power is within you.

Open your eyes, your heart, and your intuition.

Forgive him. Love him.
But please don't sacrifice your happiness for his.
You have one "go 'round" in this life. Live your life.
Forgive him. Love him.
But please don't lose the values I raised you with:
Compassion, kindness, generosity, empathy, happiness,
love, authenticity,
And honesty will never place you on the wrong path.
Forgive him, yes. Love him, yes.
But please do not model your life after him.
Manifest your highest potential.
You were born to serve HIM not him.

My poem was inspired by an article in a national magazine that shared pieces of my daughter's story. The journalist had insight into some of my daughter's struggles after spending a significant amount of time interviewing Amber at her father's home. Soon after the article was published, I contacted the journalist and asked her if she knew any of the backstory as to why my teenage daughter was experiencing severe anxiety and chronic depression.

She stated that she was unaware of any backstory. She also noted, "I have to tell you, of all the teenagers I interviewed for this story, your daughter appeared to be the most fragile. I was truly afraid for her."

"Do you know why she seemed the most fragile?" was my response.

"No. I do not."

"Because since the fall of 2010, all my daughter wanted was to live with the parent who was her primary caregiver since birth. That parent was me. I fought hard. She fought hard. But, our constant pleadings fell on deaf ears. The family court system did everything in its power to keep us apart. My daughter displayed serious health issues as a result of being kept in her father's home against her will. I have medical records stating as such. I personally have witnessed more than seven symptoms that several trauma experts identify as indicators of trauma. Those indicators did not appear until Amber was court-ordered out of our family home. And, not one person charged with the responsibility of protecting her connected the dots."

I was frustrated at this point as I saw this journalist as being one more person who noticed a red flag but failed to follow through with her concerns.

"Both your daughter and your former husband did mention you, but neither would give me permission to interview you for the article," was her response.

"Do you know why? Can you think of why they did not want you to speak with me before the article went to print?"

"No, I do not know. But, since they would not permit me to speak with you, I opted not to print anything they stated about you."

"Thank you for not printing anything that you were not permitted to confirm as being a truth."

At that point, the journalist stated that she had been on the phone too long with me and that she had colleagues waiting for her. The call ended there. To this day, I will never know what was stated about me. But truly, it does not matter. This experience has taught me many things. One of which is to not worry about another person's statements concerning me. It is none of my business what other people think. It is my responsibility, however, to not fall into the trap of always needing to defend myself. The book *The Four Agreements* by Don Miguel Ruiz taught me not to take anything personally. Since reading *The Four Agreements* more than once, I have learned to let other people's opinions of me go. My spiritual lesson was to let so many other things go. I no longer felt the need to speak with my former husband in a quest to convince him to respect my role in our children's lives. I learned to respect Ned's spiritual journey and his attention to his wounds within his timeframe. I had to learn how to do the same for my children as well.

Matthew and Amber have their own individual spiritual truths and their own personal experiences that have been far different from my own. They will learn to heal their wounds within their own timeframes. If I do not want to be judged, I cannot judge. I can neither speed up another's healing nor can I force another human to place the well-being of a child above their own needs. We each have our own spiritual journey. I have learned that what works best for me is not what works best for all. It is my choice to lead with love. It can only be my hope *and my prayer* that Ned, Matthew, and Amber also learn to lead with love.

"I need some place simple where I can live and something only you can give, and that's faith and trust and peace while we're alive. And there's one poor child who saved the world — and there's ten million more who probably could, if we all just stopped and said a prayer for them." ~Goo Goo Dolls, "Better Days."

Chapter 2
Forgiveness: Prepare To Make Nice

"I'm not ready to make nice,
I'm not ready to back down,
I'm still mad as hell
And I don't have time to go 'round and 'round and
'round."
~Dixie Chicks, "Not Ready To Make Nice."

The act of forgiveness and the emotion known as anger can be very controversial topics. I reference the song "Not Ready To Make Nice," co-written and performed by American country music band Dixie Chicks, because it represents female empowerment to me. The hit song, released in 2006, became my fighting song when I was angered by injustice. According to an article in *Rolling Stone*, the song was written at an emotional time for the band, after their music had been blacklisted because of their political views. Another report about the song describes it as having a "universal interpretation." And, as far as I am concerned, the song does.

The song references anger and, in particular, a form of anger that leads to hate: "It's a sad, sad story when a mother will teach her daughter that she ought to hate a perfect stranger, And how in the world can the words that I said send somebody so over the edge that they'd write me a letter sayin' that I better shut up and sing or my life will be over…"

The band members were reported to be angry for being banned from country music radio stations. However, their ability to openly speak truth to power is the female empowerment piece that drew me into the lyric. As I reflect over the last few decades, I recognize the several times that my own anger got the best of me. In order for me to evolve spiritually, I had to learn to dig deep to reflect and explore how to best define "healthy anger" and what defined "self-destructive anger." In order to move forward within my own journey, I had to learn to let go of the emotion known as hate as well as any form of destructive anger. It may sound trite, but I achieved this through prayer. The process was slow. There were times I would pray incessantly. There were times I would give up on my faith and on prayer. Then something would happen — something more than a coincidence —something serendipitous.

I came to understand that there is such a thing as healthy anger. I can safely assume that it was the healthy form of anger that inspired Dr. Martin Luther King Jr. in leading the civil rights movement. I can safely assume it was the same form of healthy anger that aroused the women's rights movement. I can assure you that it is the same form of healthy anger that has polarized survivors of domestic abuse to become outspoken advocates and led to the formation of a separate but equally important movement: The Protective Mother's Movement. I cannot speak for all protective mothers, but I do believe that along with grief and sorrow, a protective mother will experience all forms of anger before she heals. Although the act of forgiveness is not for everyone, I have come to understand how it can play a significant role in being grounded within healthy anger.

Sheryl Sandberg, co-author of *The New York Times* bestseller *Option B*, often refers to being stuck in the emotion of grief as being "in the void." I would like to include the inability to forgive as well as the self-destructive form of anger as also being "in the void." Forgiveness, anger, and grief are each a process in and of themselves. The trajectory of healing and moving forward in one's spiritual journey is not a straight line. It is a squiggly line that shoots straight up, plunges down sharply, and circles "round and 'round and 'round. It's too late to make it right."

Is it too late to make it right? The answer is yes and no. It is too late to replace what was lost, taken, stolen, and any other appropriate verbiage that a grieving mother may use when telling her story. However, it is never too late to say "I am sorry," "Please forgive me," "I was wrong," or "I forgive you." It is never too late to say "I love you." It is never too late to repair something that, in hindsight, you regret doing or saying. My point is this: Once the anger has passed, it is never too late to make nice. Forgiveness is a powerful tool. I had to learn to forgive myself and to forgive those who became obstacles to the relationship between my children and me. My hope and prayer is that in forgiveness I can find peace, joy, healing, and a transition from a person who had to survive to a person who can and will thrive.

One would have to make a conscientious decision to make nice. I understand that this is a process and something not everyone can do. All I can say is that I have been fortunate enough to have acquired the gift to forgive. However, I must warn you that with forgiveness, you may experience a form of amnesia. This amnesia serves a purpose. When memories are too painful to replay over and over in your subconscious, the brain may file them away until a trigger brings the experience back to your conscience mind. There are several examples that I could list. These following memories abruptly resurface at any given moment and on any given day. I allow myself to process the memory. I attempt to make sense of it, because hindsight is always 20/20. Then I place the burden of the atrocity onto the perpetrator, and I simply let it go. Do not misunderstand: I do not forget. Instead, I just file the memory or thought into a bin that no longer warrants my attention. I remind myself that my focus and my energy – today – is best spent on the here and now. The following are just a small sampling of those files I no longer open up.

"Dad said that when he gets his money back, he is going to buy himself a new Ford Mustang," were the words spoken by Matthew one weekend afternoon.

Money back? Did my children's father lend someone some money? No. He is not the type to lend money. What is Matthew talking about? Obviously, he is parroting back something he heard his father say. Hm. Not important.

I clearly remember my inner dialogue after hearing my son's enthusiasm at the thought of his father someday buying himself a fancy sports car. It made no sense, so I let that memory go until 2016, the year my youngest was graduating from high school. It was that spring that Matthew posted on his Instagram account how proud he was of his hardworking father who sacrificed so much to work seven days a week to finally reward himself with a custom-built 2016 Ford Mustang. That was when the ah-hah moment hit. "His money back" meant no longer being court-ordered to pay child support from the time my parental rights were stripped from me in the winter of 2014 and I was the one court-ordered to pay child support for the next two years. Clearly, my child support factored into Ned affording a $50,000 vehicle. Rather than getting angry, I flipped the narrative and gave myself credit for buying a sports car for my children's father. Oddly, I found some satisfaction in that.

"After we sell the house, do you mind if I take a portion of my proceeds to buy Matthew an ATV?" Ned said before we even finalized our 2006 divorce.

Sure. Go ahead. Do what you want. After all, it is your money. I personally am focusing on providing a roof over my head for the kids and me, but sure, do what you want.

I had been caught off-guard, and I had been completely naïve when I did not consider Amber in Ned's odd request. It took a few weeks before Amber lamented, "All I do on the weekends with dad is watch Matthew ride his ATV with our cousins. I get so bored, mom."

Like a bullet between the eyes, it struck me. Ned's favoritism toward Matthew was one the several reasons why a year's worth of counseling failed to reconcile our marriage. Ned grew up in a household where the females ranked lower in the hierarchy. I witnessed several times how my former father-in-law treated my former mother-in-law like a servant. It was extremely unsettling to observe. Quite frankly, their relationship scared me. In them, I saw us. A prisoner to old-fashioned gender roles was not what I had hoped for when I uttered the words, "to honor and obey." Now, through the interactions of father and child, I was observing the same patriarchal value system being repeated in the lives our children. Advocating for Amber would soon become one of the topics that would label our co-parenting relationship as "high-conflict."

"You abandoned the children. You ruined their lives. I hope you feel proud of yourself," was a common opening statement in emails Ned sent to me.

To create havoc in our lives, Ned often used the communication tool referred to as "co-parenting emails" to chip away at my self-esteem. In hindsight, the emails were just another way to stir the pot. I would get irate when I read them. The irritation would quickly turn to anger. I started to treat Ned the way he treated me thinking that would make him see how unfair and judgmental he was being. If he understood how I felt, then he would change. Or so I thought. The strategy immediately backfired. Once my thoughts and reactions were captured in email format, it gave Ned the tangible evidence he needed to frame me as being difficult to deal with. Over the months and years, I cannot recall all of the names I was called, and all of the things I was accused of doing. Suffice it to say 90-percent of the email exchanges were toxic. I have since shredded the thousands and thousands of papers downloaded from my computer.

"Save the emails," I was advised by a domestic abuse advocate. "Compile them in a three-ring-binder," I was advised by an assistant that worked for the district attorney's office. In hindsight, those pieces of advice were a complete waste of time, money, and energy. The family court personnel did not care. They never asked to see evidence of coercive control. Instead, they did just the opposite. They dismissed or ignored all evidence of coercive control. When I sought out legal advice regarding harassment, coercive control, and contempt of court orders, I was advised by more than one person to "let it all go." I was informed more than once that to advocate for myself and to stand up for my rights was to risk being labeled as "uncooperative."

"He will only retaliate if you hold him accountable. Do not file a motion for contempt. It will only make it worse," was the advice I often got. Then I was warned that if I got angry, my anger could be reframed as a display of emotional instability.

What? How can any of this be possible? None of this makes sense.

To better understand how possible it is, I recommend reading Janie McQueen's book *Hanging On By My Fingernails: Surviving the New Divorce Gamesmanship, and How a Scratch Can Land You in Jail.* I was given a free copy and read the first half. I did not finish reading the book because, well, it was making me too angry, and at that point in my life, I was getting very tired of that emotion. My priority was on being the light my children needed to see. Their father displayed enough anger and irrational behaviors. I felt our children needed me to be the counterbalance to his negative energies. Children absorb what a parent emits. If a parent suffers

31

from depression, it is more than likely a child will become depressed. If a parent suffers from severe anxiety, it is very likely that a child will also become anxious. Ned and I were told by several counselors that the children will pick up the energy that you give off. We were also told by a few counselors that it was not the divorce in and of itself that would harm the children. Instead, it was how we would choose to handle the divorce. Emphasis on the words *choose* and *handle*.

The pressure on me was constant. I felt I had to be the yin to Ned's yang. I understood that he was resentful. After all, I was the one who chose not to be the doting, submissive, 1950s-style housewife. And I was the one who filed for the divorce. I understand the one who is being divorced is usually the one who holds the most resentment. What no one knew about me was the divorce sent me into a situational depression: The last thing I ever wanted was to be divorced. I know it was the last thing Ned wanted. He had already been married and divorced once before. However, that experience — even when coupled with yearlong, weekly marriage counseling session — did not prompt Ned to work on our marriage. He wanted someone to "fix" me, and then our marriage would be okay. After more than 50 counseling sessions, it was clear that Ned took no responsibility for our marriage failing.

At one point, a former counselor of mine contacted me to tell me that Ned had called her office and asked her to "medicate me." She stated, "I typically would not bother you with this, but I felt you needed to know this. Your husband called me and asked me to prescribe you medication so that you would not divorce him."

Seriously? How did he get your number? Has he ever done anything like this before?

"Yes, he did call me. I thought it was odd for him to call me. No, this was the first time he has ever called me. He sounded desperate. I thought you should know."

Ok. I am asking you, and I need you to be perfectly honest with me. Do you think I need to be medicated?

"No," she answered. "No, you don't. Trust me. If I thought that you would benefit from medication, I would tell you. But, you do not need to be prescribed medication. You are such a strong woman.

Do not doubt yourself for one minute. There is nothing clinically wrong with you."

Another one of those memories I set aside came years after our divorce.

"Natalie and I want to get married. She has two children close in age to Amber and Matthew. We live together now. We want to create a family without having you involved."

Those were the words Ned uttered to explain the 2012 court petition to terminate my parental rights. My present husband insisted we hire a lawyer to protect my rights as a mother.

It is not possible, I thought. *I have done nothing wrong. How can this even be possible? Who petitions the court to terminate a mother's right to be involved in her children's lives?*

One in two marriages end in divorce. People divorce and remarry all the time without terminating a parent's rights in order to "start a new family." The whole idea sounded completely insane to me. At the time, I was a full-time university student in the process of completing my bachelor's degree. I was commuting an hour each way to class four days a week, working on weekends, interning at a local nonprofit, and now being asked to find money to procure a lawyer to defend my right to remain in my children's lives.'

Insane. Totally insane, I thought.

From the time I was served court papers to the time of trial, 14 months had gone by. Those 14 months were an all-out slugfest, as Brene Brown would say in her TED Talk video, "The Power of Vulnerability." In the end, I lost the battle, but I won back my life.

The aftermath, grief, and reactionary suicide attempt brought me to a place of reckoning. I had to let all of the anger, resentment, and negative energy go. It was no longer my cross to bear. The universe provided me with a support system and a well of resilience like I have never experienced before. With faith, prayer, and a determination to rise above all those who directly and indirectly chose to harm my children and me, I found forgiveness. It took four years, but I found it.

~~~~~~~~~~~

And, with forgiveness, I found joy again. I was able to laugh again. Smile again. The Earth took on a whole new appearance. Flowers and butterflies were more beautiful than ever before. Every breath, every accomplishment, every sensation took on a whole new feeling. I was alive. I was alive, and I was determined to enjoy every second of every minute of each day.

He took my home, my retirement, my savings, my good credit rating, my self-esteem, my confidence, my voice, my worldly possessions — sold to pay off legal debt. He took my time with my children, my children's childhood; in a nutshell, he took my whole life.

But I lived. I did not die. There were times when I literally had to take my day one minute at a time. There were times that I wanted to just disappear — buy a one-way ticket anywhere in the world and start my life over. But I held tight to faith and prayer. *All things are possible with God,* I would remind myself.

I prayed incessantly. Daily I prayed to Archangel Michael to protect both Amber and Matthew. I prayed to Archangel Raphael to heal us from the trauma we experienced. I prayed to Archangel Ariel to fill our lives with abundance — not wealth, but abundance of good health, peace, love, joy, forgiveness, and support systems.

I understand that the harm done to my children was not my cross to bear. My faith assures me that those who knowingly set in motion the obstacles that deteriorated my relationship with my children will someday meet their maker. Karma is the action of receiving the energy back that you put out. I have made great efforts to perform random acts of kindness. I have a very different approach to my life that I do not think I would have if I had not gone through such atrocities.

I would often recite prayers taught to me by one of my former bosses. I smile thinking of her because she instantly became a very close confidante and friend. Sophia is, without a doubt, an Earth angel put on my path at exactly the right time. She taught me the following prayers. The first is a paraphrase of the ho'oponopono healing prayer, a Hawaiian prayer to promote any healing process. Trauma or estrangement is a sufficient reason to incorporate this prayer into your practice. I often used this prayer to communicate to my children through the energy of the universe:

Matthew and Amber,
I am so, so sorry.
I forgive you. Please forgive me.
I love you. We are one.

In its simplest form, the ho'oponopono meditation is four phases:

I love you.
I'm sorry.
Please forgive me.
Thank you.

Another meditation prayer that I found effective is this: "Thy will be done through me for the highest good of all and for the true manifestation of my purpose."

With all due respect to the band the Dixie Chicks, I am finally at a place in my life journey that I can confidently say, I am ready to make nice.

Chapter 3
Healing Begins When You Speak Your Truth: Be Brave

"You can be amazing.
You can turn a phrase into a weapon or a drug.
You can be an outcast, or the backlash
To somebody's lack of love,
Or you can start speaking up."
~Sara Bareilles, "Brave"

As you have probably concluded by now, music is therapeutic for me. I drew upon several healing outlets in order to survive the new divorce gamesmanship; however, music has been and always will be among the most powerful. I know it was also therapeutic for my daughter Amber as well; she felt as drawn to the lyrics in "Fix You" by the group Coldplay as I was to Sara Bareilles's song "Brave." But due to our estrangement, I never knew why Amber found Coldplay's lyrics healing for her. Why Coldplay? Why the lyric, "Lights will guide you home." Was this a reference to her being held captive in a home that did not feel like home to her? That was the thought that brought my heart the most pain.

A few years after the divorce, I found myself entering into very hostile territory often referred to as "the revolving door of family court." The environment was at once completely strange to me as well as oddly familiar. Derogatory insults and judgments regarding my personhood from Ned had become all too common. Growing up, my stepfather was known to berate us children into obedience and submission. But I was a child then. As an adult, I thought I could form boundaries to keep angry and hostile personalities from affecting me. Until I travelled through the halls and rooms of family court. There, I learned the hard way that being civilized to one another was not how the "game" was played.

According to Barry Goldstein, author of *The Quincy Solution*, the price tag for American taxpayers to cover the cost of the family court system's disregard of protective mothers during contested court procedures is $500 billion annually. The mothers who choose to leave a toxic or abusive relationship more often than not become victim to a series of court processes that leave them broke, traumatized, and riddled with chronic health problems. "Verbal, emotional, and psychological abuse are forms of abuse far more common than physical abuse," Goldstein writes. "They serve to reduce the victim's self-esteem and punish her for failing to obey." Additionally, Goldstein asserts, "We repeatedly see cases in which the father who had little involvement with the children during the relationship seeks custody in response to the mother's decision to escape."

As I connected with other protective mothers located all over the globe, I came to realize that the divorce court process has targeted thousands and thousands of us. I was not alone. And neither were Matthew and Amber. Several sources indicate an estimated 58,000 United States children annually are taken from the primary caregiver's home — the primary caregiver usually being the mother.

The lawyers, guardians-ad-litem or GALs, and judges became an extension of the abuse. To have them join in on the harsh personal attacks turned me into a person I never knew I could be again: the frightened young child I once was. I slowly became self-conscious, a nervous wreck, forgetful, and easily distracted. I became scared and sought emotional safety anywhere I could find it. I became the child who felt unsafe in her own home — the child who, no matter what, was always guilty of something she did not do. Unconsciously, I was reverting back to life with my stepfather, a very controlling man who ruled our home using tactics such as verbal berating, corporal punishment, and much worse. He had a habit of barging into the bathroom when he knew I was in the process of undressing. In hindsight, and through a lot of therapy, I came to realize that in marrying Ned, I had chosen a man whose behavior closely resembled that of my stepfather. And to this day, anyone expressing anger and rage toward me brings back those long-dormant childhood fears.

The attacks on my character as a mother and as a person were disempowering. These attacks came from several sources such as the opposing attorneys, my attorney, and the court-appointed GAL, just to name a few. I soon realized that I used to be quite empowered and very capable. I actually had accomplished a lot in my life. How could I possibly regress to the introverted, helpless child I once was? I have been told by others that what I was experiencing was referred to as judicial abuse, and as such, it is not uncommon for a woman to exhibit signs of stress and trauma known as complex PTSD. As the continuation of family court proceedings took more and more of my resources, I became more and more disempowered. This downward spiral of both my physical and mental health left me searching for healthy options to regain a foothold to return to the leader I once was. As such, I found myself particularly drawn to the lyrics from Sara Bareilles's "Brave." I reminded myself that I had met similar challenges before and I survived. If I was able to rise above gossip and character assassination before, I could certainly manage the latest onslaught of criticism and false accusations.

"Everybody's been there.
Everybody's been stared down by the enemy,
Fallen for the fear and done some disappearing,
Bowed down to the mighty,
Don't run, stop holding your tongue..."

I reminded myself that I have spoken truth to power before and could certainly do it again. The first time was back in the year 2000. I had been told that an allegation was made by a young lady who was experiencing severe anxiety and depression. She was having flashbacks of being alone with my stepfather and alleged he may have abused her at the tender age of five. When I first heard these allegations, my whole body went numb. I was in shock, and I felt responsible. I blamed myself, believe that somehow by keeping the family secret a secret, another young child had been harmed. Then I panicked, wondering how many other children he harmed.

Ruth Collins

"Your history of silence won't do you any good.
Did you think it would?
Let your words be anything but empty.
Why don't you tell them the truth?"

The second time I chose to speak truth to power was when I approached United Church of Christ officials asking about the ethical, moral, and professional responsibility of one of their ministers. After my divorce, I became quite vulnerable. I am not excusing my part of having involved myself with my church minister, but at the time when our relationship shifted from platonic to romantic, Pastor Ralph had vowed to me that our relationship had been "sanctioned" by his superiors.

What I later found out was faith leaders have an obligation and an ethical responsibility to maintain healthy boundaries with their parishioners. Ralph, who had been my minister for the prior six years, was also newly divorced. Since he had convinced me that our relationship was sanctioned by his overseers, I had no reason to believe we were behaving in a way that would affect his career. However, Ralph slowly shifted his story of our relationship being sanctioned. First, he asked me to stop attending church services with my children. I should have been suspect when Ralph also stated that it would be best for all involved if I kept our relationship a secret. I trusted him and felt that his request was easy enough since my childhood was full of family secrets. In hindsight, I was raised to protect the guilty as well as the innocent by keeping secrets. Once I discovered that Ralph had been deceiving me all along, I felt that same shock I had endured when I heard of other possible victims of my stepfather. After years of counseling and healing, I realize now that none of this was my fault: The only person responsible for deception, abuse, or professional misconduct is the perpetrator.

Being victimized by a parent figure was traumatizing. Being victimized by a faith leader that I knew and trusted for more than eight years was also traumatizing, but the worst trauma was having my former spouse petition the court to take away my parental rights. I cannot discern if it was the back-to-back experiences from being a victim of clergy abuse with then being a victim of domestic abuse by proxy, or if the process of being marginalized and removed from the lives of my children was in and of itself enough to propel me, as a protective mother, into a state of mind where suicide seemed to be my only choice.

Let me be clear: Suicide should never be your option. It is true, as the saying goes, that suicide is a permanent solution to a temporary problem. My head spins, recalling the day I was informed that I was no longer legally permitted to be my children's mother. Let that thought resonate in your mind. The month was January. The year was 2014. I was hit by the perfect storm: the news that my parental rights had been taken from me, the argument between myself and my present husband that soon followed, and the crisis call that I made to my former counselor who, as I recall, started to yell into the phone. As I have mentioned before, anger and rage are triggers for me. Trigger. Trigger. Trigger. Trauma. Then the thought, *is this going to push Amber over the edge? How do I explain my sudden absence from my children's lives? Who will advocate for their safety, medical and academic needs? When will I ever see them again? What about other family members? How is this at all possible? I did nothing wrong. That is, unless being a protective mother who validated my daughter's disclosures of maltreatment was wrong somehow.*

The tsunami of emotional pain broke me. I ran into my bedroom, grabbed what I had for leftover pain medication from a prior surgery, and swallowed it, following it up with a glass of wine. Suddenly, a voice bellowed within my head, "That was a stupid thing to do. Do you realize how dangerous that is?" I came to my senses and calmly asked my husband to call 911. What happened next was surreal. Being in a state of emotional shock, I vaguely remember the EMTs. I was embarrassed, as I recognized one of them as a member of our community. They were kind and compassionate.

How often do you see this? How many calls do you get from mothers who want to end their lives because the thought of never seeing their children again is just too much to bear? How many?

In the ER, I was given an awful, black, tar-like liquid to drink to absorb the toxins in my stomach. I remember the looks from the staff ranged from compassion to indifference, with everything in between.

41

I was emotionally unsound. I remember telling them my present husband was abusive. Anger. Rage. Triggers. I knew in my heart that Joseph was hurting, too. He stood by my side and watched helplessly for four years the destruction of the mother-child bond. He had borrowed from his own retirement fund to retain our last lawyer, the lawyer who promised to fight a hard fight only later to show up in the courtroom and inform the presiding judge that he failed to prepare for trial. My jaw had dropped. In the courtroom with me for support were my sister, my brother, and two domestic violence advocates — one from the state I now live in and one from the state in which all of the family court drama was unfolding. None of them could believe what they had just heard.

"I am sorry, your honor. I don't understand. This is the busiest that I have ever been. I have just been too busy to prepare for trial."

"Well, you had plenty of time to prepare, counselor. The trial will go on," was the judge's retort.

That was the December of 2013. Even though the judge had promised a decision within the next two weeks, he did not follow through.

Between trial and judgment, I had been invited to join a public forum through which my prior home state was collecting public testimony regarding the effectiveness of its family court system. There had been years of complaints, so the state government had put together a panel committee to hear public input. The hope was the panel would spark consideration of reform options to improve the system, or so I was told by a leader of a local grassroots advocacy group.

Only when I arrived to share my experiences did I learn that the judge who presided over my family's court proceeding the month before was a prominent member of this committee. He recognized me a few minutes after I began speaking. Rather than recusing himself, he stopped me mid-sentence and told me to sit down. And I did. That was the 14th of January, 2014. Two days later, when he signed the final judgment of our trial — the trial determining whether or not I would retain my parental rights — he was clever enough to note at the bottom of the first page of our trial judgment that the outcome had nothing to do with my public testimony regarding the effectiveness of the state's family court system.

His judgment had been the final straw. He broke me.

The emotional pain and torment were too much to bear. Then, in a flash, there was my present husband: A good man. My rock. One of the biggest cheerleaders I had even known. I could not give up on us or on me. God put me on this Earth for a reason. Maybe the voice inside my head that told me to ask Joseph to call 911 was the voice of my Higher Power. My purpose for being here and for going through hell on Earth was to serve a much greater purpose. I needed to live in order to find out what that mission was.

I will never forget the kindness of the doctor who spoke with me the day after being admitted to the mental health ward of the local hospital. He asked me what happened — why I had become an inpatient. I unloaded the whole story of what took place in family court and the outcome of the trial to terminate my parental rights. I will never forget his reaction as I finished retelling the series of events that led to me being removed from the lives of my children. He looked almost relieved as well as disgusted. He stated that he would recommend I be discharged home as soon as possible as long as I made one promise.

What? Sure! Anything. Just please let me go home. I want to be with my husband. I know he is going to miss the children, too. He has grown to love them as his own. He has to be suffering as well, and he is alone right now.

"I want you to promise me that when this whole thing is over and you are feeling strong enough, you will contact all of the people responsible for landing you here; and tell them what you told me. Tell them that none of the process or the judgment was ever in the best interest of the children. They need to know how much their decisions and actions are harming people."

After seven years of dealing with coercive control, a topic that I had never heard of before I lived through it, his words were the most validating and supportive ones I had ever heard. Up until that point, I had been made to feel as if I was the first mother to go through this process. Yet the doctor was responding as if he had heard of this process of maternal deprivation before — perhaps over and over again.

43

More than four years have passed since my hospitalization. There is not a day that goes by when I do not practice some form of self-care. I encourage others to practice self-care on a daily basis as well. Like insulin to a diabetic, acts of self-care have maintained my present-day good health. I have diagnosed myself as "no longer the same." I recognize that trauma has permanently changed me. I am gentler with me. I am more forgiving and loving to me. I focus on health and wellness every day, and I am grateful that I have such a supportive husband.

And, just as important, I have become an outspoken children's rights advocate. Doors have opened that I never even realized were possible. I am so grateful to be alive. Every day is a gift. Every day I feel more empowered, more driven, and brave. Speaking truth to power is now my weapon of choice. Practicing three random acts of kindness to every insult to my soul is my strategy. Every protective mother I meet in person or on-line inspires me.

"You can be amazing. You can turn into a weapon or a drug."

This may sound cheesy, but that is okay. My choice of weapon is truth, and my drug is love. A fellow protective mother from Georgia, Melonda, has coined the war cry "love wins." We communicate through social media and support each other by sharing our "love wins" photos and memes. It is that kind of sentiment that empowers a man, woman, or child to be brave. Yes, Melonda, let's model for all to see: Love wins.

"Honestly, I want to see you be brave."

Chapter 4
Warrior Mothers: Your Scars Make You Beautiful

"But there's a hope
That's waiting for you in the dark.
You should know
You're beautiful just the way you are.
And you don't have to change a thing.
The world can change its heart.
No scars to your beautiful,
We're stars and we're beautiful."
~Alessia Cara, "Scars to Your Beautiful"

It is often stated by the mothers within my tribe that a husband who loses his wife is called a widower, a wife who loses her husband is called a widow, and children who lose their parents are called orphans, but there is no word for a mother who loses her child. She has no label.

Mothers deprived of their children lose children to life rather than to death; therefore, there is no universal word within our language to describe us. Without a name or a description, we are left misunderstood. Alone. We are left without a roadmap for healing. Broken. We are scarred. And no one seems to know how to heal us. Our healing comes from several resources. Regardless of how we chose to heal, I firmly believe it is those healed scars that make us more human and more beautiful.

For some grief-stricken mothers, a variety of unhealthy or negative options such as self-harm, isolation, alcohol abuse, or self-medicating seem the only way to cope, but all of these exacerbate anxiety and depression. Many of these mothers eventually become physically and mentally disabled, unable to hold down a full-time job due to the trauma from losing a child.

Others have extensive support systems that provide more healthy options and positive tools. These support systems are the key for moving beyond trauma and toward a journey that is full of joy as well as physical and emotional stability. Joy and good health become the foundation for surviving trauma. These tools, over time, point survivors toward a life where they can thrive again. It is a beautiful transition to experience; I liken it to a rebirth. Just as a caterpillar breaks free from the darkness of a tightly closed chrysalis in order to become the most beautiful butterfly, a mother who has lost her children through coercive control can transform into one of the most beautiful souls that walks this Earth.

For me, there is nothing more beautiful than a person who has experienced the worst pain she could humanly withstand and yet still finds the strength to support a stranger who lives thousands of miles away. Case in point: I received a message from a woman in Hawaii via social media. This newly found friend openly shared her thoughts as to how similar our paths seem to be. Like me, she lost her child through the process of coercive control. Our connection deepened as she reached out to me on Thanksgiving Day 2017.

"Aloha Ruth. It is almost noon here on Maui, Thanksgiving Day. I decided to write you as I sense from your Facebook posts that we seem to have a similar take on things. I decided a long time ago to work to remain in joy and gratitude as much as possible in the face of my own experience with the custody-abuse darkness. The last week or so have been very peaceful. I have once again been able to sit quietly in meditation every day for the recommended 15 minutes. The trauma stole that gift for many, many, many, years and so I have really been enjoying the fruits of that time these last days. Until last night, when the email came in from my almost 16-year-old daughter. Her father and stepmother allow her to talk to me about an hour every other week."

My newfound friend trails off as she begins to detail the emotional rollercoaster surrounding the holidays. Before she devoted those 15 minutes a day to meditation, the holidays were full of angst and unknowns. Will she see her child? Will she hear from her child? Will she be allowed to exchange gifts with her child? Her description of the chaos that surrounded the holidays was too familiar to me: In a game of power and control, withholding a child from a mother during holidays is the most painful power-play the other parent can perform. Those who abuse the mother of their children understand this, and this game of "Will You or Won't You" spend time with your child ramps up and can blindside you. Having one's hopes up only to then have them come crashing down is far worse than knowing you will not see the children at all. I know from personal experience that this game is heartbreaking for the adult: I cannot begin to fathom how the children must feel. My friend finishes her post with, "I am sure it falls under the heading of gas-lighting. It brings judgment and isolation on the mother because we recognize we sound crazy trying to respond to craziness."

In other words, when pulled into the vortex of power and control, we cannot help absorbing some of the low-vibrating, negative energy that comes from anyone trying to control us. When we attempt to explain to the well-meaning family and friends who ask, "Will you spend time with your children this holiday?" that we do not know, we sound crazy.

My response to my friend was to assure her that I understood. I also gave her some insight as to how I have learned to deal with what I cannot control. For far too long, my survival strategy was to expect chaos and attempt to preempt chaos by trying to figure out what was in Ned's head. After years and years of failing to know what Ned's "game-play du jour" might be, I had no choice but to hope for the best and expect nothing. My friend Sophia taught me this rule of the Universe: Open your heart, set your intention, and then let go of the outcome. For me, it was one of the most difficult life lessons to learn. And to be completely frank, I wish I had learned that lesson a long time ago. My own childhood trauma had given me the illusion that to control all aspects of your life was to avoid being targeted. Control freaks and over achievers as we are sometimes called — fool ourselves into thinking we can control all aspects of our lives: Plan ahead. Set a goal. Be organized. Control. Control. Control. This is one of the biggest lies we tell ourselves. In truth, we can only control us. We cannot control how another person chooses to behave. If an unhealthy person chooses to withhold children from their loving and nurturing mother, then there truly is not a whole lot that mother can do. If you think the family court system would intervene, then you are sadly mistaken. The system cannot be bothered with personality issues: As I have been told, "We *cannot make him be a nice person.*"

Back to my friend's communications.

I explained that I have learned not to take any of these "will you or won't you" games personally. Too many weekends, birthdays, and holidays have been spent without my own children. The only way to remain sane was to never expect to see them. When I did get to see them, it was a huge event. I took photographs whenever I could. I took photographs for the very same reason every parent takes photographs, but I also took them because I never knew when I would see my children again. I never shared those thoughts with Matthew and Amber. To this day, they have no idea how much I kept buried deep inside. But there was a reason why our time together was captured by cell-phone or digital camera. It was because I was never promised a tomorrow with my children. My children and I were never protected by the court, which focused only on the letter of the law and not on fostering a healthy bond between mother and child.

Looking back, I know there was a reason I took them on a cruise vacation in April of 2010. I knew that the December 2009 court petition by their father was potentially just the beginning of what I had been warned about: Some hands-off fathers decide to petition the court for full custody of the children. Well-advertised fathers' rights attorneys openly boast in their marketing that they can assure their clients will get out of child support payments by simply filing for sole custody. Is this really so different from a slave owner auctioning off the child of a slave for profit? After having had this experience, I better understood the very personal tragedies of the atrocity that was the American slave trade.

After a divorce is finalized, the only way for an abusive person to continue controlling the mother of his children is to take the very thing that brings her the most joy time spent nurturing, loving, and being an active participant in raising her children. Several survivors of these tactics have turned into activists, and some have created nonprofits to support victims of the family courts. The Women's Coalition, based out of California, has a Facebook page by the same name devoted to "raising awareness about the systemic discrimination leading to the loss of and inability to protect children, and are creating a new system which will stop judges from taking children from good mothers and punishing them for trying to keep or protect them." At present, the coalition has more than 17,000 followers, and its administrator has published an event entitled "Faces of the Crisis." The event is "a compilation of women whose children were taken and/or not protected by family court judges." Their stories are similar to my story and that of my friend from Hawaii.

Back to my friend's response to me.

"I will treasure the gem you offered, 'I take nothing personally.' I humbly admire you for that because I know the amount of work it takes to get to that place. The pain of separation from our children is so deep; it takes incredible work and energy to get to that place. Have you found that as they got older, in mid-to-late teens, it got a bit easier? It has for me. I often wonder if it is part of the developmental individualization process. I have instinctually known how close I needed to be and sensed when she was becoming more viable as her own human being…I'm actually grateful that time is coming because it means I am less subjected to the crazy controlling from the father and stepmother. Truthfully, if I weren't so committed to the well-being of her soul, I would have bailed long ago. But I have seen it as the responsibility of being her mother that I withstand their BS. It certainly has made me stronger as I learned to withstand it. Part of my Thanksgiving gratitude today was the recognition that it does not hurt my spirit and soul the way it did for so many years. This past year in particular has brought more relief than at any point in the past."

I thanked my friend for sharing her experience with me, and I assured her that I was also in agreement: We are both at a very similar place within our own personal journey. I did not go into detail, but I also felt as if this past year was a lot less tumultuous than the one before. I was no longer court-ordered to communicate with Ned. Both children were over the age of 18 and were situated in a place where their own personal decisions and choices were the reason for our estrangement. I say that without blame or judgment. Instead, I recognize that children of the same age group even within a healthy home environment would be becoming more self-actualized and independent. Matthew and Amber were robbed of that. Knowing that I continually made efforts to communicate with Amber and Matthew lessened any sense of failure I may have felt when they were young and unable to understand the decisions being made without their input or without any thought to how they felt. Now that they are both in their early twenties, they have — to a greater extent than ever before — control over their lives.

I have told them several times that my love for them remains unconditional and all I ever wanted for them was to be happy, healthy, and safe. I had to open my heart, set an intention, and let go of the outcome. My intention was for us to be whole again. My intention was for us to heal together. But that was where I had to learn to let go. Letting go does not mean not caring or praying for them. Letting go, for me, means being free from worry, from fear, and from anxiety over those things that I cannot control. Letting go means freedom. Freedom for my soul. Freedom to have my life back. Freedom to heal. Freedom to connect with true joy. Letting go was the gift I gave to myself.

There's a hope that's waiting for you in the dark. You should know you're beautiful just the way you are. And you don't have to change a thing, the world can change its heart. No scars to your beautiful, we're stars and we're beautiful.

"I've continued to search on this inexplicable path of family court who has been working to respond to it in a different way. I didn't want to be angry or broken. I wanted to become stronger and better because of this. It's been hard to find others who held this position — so many held in the grip of trauma and anger…It was scary when I heard of others who gave up and took their own lives. I am grateful every single day for the GRACE which allowed me to survive," my friend continued.

Her compliment regarding my spiritual growth made me smile; however, her comment about other mothers who gave up and "took their own lives" made me feel a bit of guilt. She did not know all of my story. She was unaware of how close I came to giving up. Other than one or two close family members, no one knew of my suicide attempt or of my overnight hospitalization once I received the judgment of our 2014 custody trial. I kept this incident close to my heart because I did not want to burden my children. If I could give the children targeted by coercive control one absolute assurance, I would tell them that none of what happened is their fault. I know Amber was made to feel responsible for reacting to trauma in a normal way. To place the blame onto a victim — especially a child — is to make the perpetrators and bystanders feel less responsible for their actions and inactions.

I then disclosed to my friend that I was in the middle of writing this memoir. I asked her permission to use her words to help share our journey.

"Yes! Of course! I would be more than happy to share anything and everything I learned and used. Helping others come through this is one of my quiet goals." She placed a heart emoji between that statement and this one: "I am so happy and grateful to know another who found a different way. When I couldn't find anyone, I decided to make Nelson Mandela my role model. Sounds funny now."

I assured her that it did not sound funny at all. I have used many strategies that others may find nontraditional, but they worked. I am alive today because of them. I am feeling joy again. I am feeling scarred but beautiful. Beautiful just like my friend in Hawaii, a woman who despite her pain and suffering has given me permission to share her insights and who has found healing within the act of giving. My friend is truly a beautiful soul. I often refer to these beautiful souls as angels on Earth. Who else but a loving and wholehearted mother would want to reach out to others and heal their pain? Who else but an angel on Earth.

No scars to your beautiful, we're stars and we're beautiful.

Unbeknownst to my friend, I had just started listening to the audio version of *The Book of JOY*, read by Douglas Abrams, Francois Chau, and Peter Francis James. The book contains conversations between His Holiness the 14th Dalia Lama and his longtime friend Archbishop Desmond Tutu. On the back cover, it is written, "they are two of the most joyful people on the planet." The Dalia Lama — to this day — lives in exile in India, and Desmond Tutu has "survived ... the soul-crushing violence of oppression." Yet despite their extremely painful experiences with loss and injustice, they are considered two of the happiest men on Earth.

51

These spiritual leaders are visionaries, and Nelson Mandela is no different. Mandela also fought against oppression and was clearly willing to lay down his life for democracy and a free society. For example, in 1964, Mandela was imprisoned for his social justice activism. One source states: "While facing the death penalty his words to the court at the end of his famous Speech from the Dock on April 20, 1964, became immortalized: "I have cherished the ideal of democratic and free society in which all persons live together in harmony and with equal opportunities. It is an ideal which I hope to live for and to achieve. But if needs be, it is an ideal for which I am prepared to die."

I know of several mothers who feel the same way about the injustice of being forced out of the lives of their children. For some, the emotional distress was too heavy a burden to bear, forcing them to give up entirely and take their lives. Others, like the members of The Women's Coalition, have made it their mission to create a new system that promotes justice and honors a mother's right to be an active participant within the life of her child.

In researching for this memoir, I came across a very timely press release on The Nelson Mandela Foundation's website from November 26, 2017. In the release, United Nations Deputy Secretary-General Amina Mohammed urges women, "Don't give up. Just remember that your life is a journey and every single step you take is part of you strengthening what you do." The title of the press release? "Women must take back the power." Intuitively, I feel as if the collective efforts of spiritual leaders and visionaries are creating a global wave of empowerment. I wholeheartedly agree with the secretary-general: women must take back the power. And the men who are virtuous and secure in their role within society — men such as the Dalai Lama, Archbishop Tutu, and Mandela — will support our efforts and dance with joy once that power is realized.

And you don't have to change a thing.
The world could change its heart.

Chapter 5
Love and Light Will Guide Our Children Home

"When you try your best,
But you don't succeed—
When you get what you want,
But not what you need.
When you feel so tired,
But you can't sleep.
Stuck in reverse...
And the tears come streaming down your face,
When you lose something you can't replace.
When you love someone,
But it goes to waste...
Could it be worse?"
~Coldplay, "Fix You."

Over the last two or three years, concerned mothers have reached out to me to express their worst fear: that their child might take their own life. These mothers have shared countless stories of their older children's behaviors, which have included cutting, drinking, and drugging. Some of these children have expressed to their mothers their desire to be dead to end their emotional pain and suffering. Suicide, for these affected children, appears to be the only path to peace. Of course, we know that is not our truth: The only path to peace is to lead with love. Love heals. Scientific research, including findings within the "Adverse Childhood Experience" studies, is validating what every protective mother already knew, that chronic exposure to toxic stress, and the trauma caused from being exposed to any form of abuse, will without a doubt take a toll on the health and wellbeing of children.

We protective mothers intuitively know that our day-to-day love and interactions with our children enable them to grow into well-adjusted, civic-minded, and empathetic adults. Conversely, a child coerced to have no contact with their mother is truly a child being emotionally and psychologically abused. Therefore, that child is at risk of adopting the behaviors of a perpetrator of some form of abuse, whether it be verbal, emotional, physical, or psychological. Hate begets hate. Love begets love. It could not be simpler. Children require authentic love in order to thrive. Children need their loving, protective mothers. Period.

Some children — like one of the brothers mentioned within the memoir *Don't Hug Your Mother* by Gareth and Fintan Murphy — never fully heal from chronic exposure to a toxic home environment or from the trauma of never knowing their own mother. Gareth and Fintan never state a mental health diagnosis; however, their memoir alludes to their older brother having some form of a psychotic break. Another example is Donna Buiso's description of her son's behavior, which is not unusual among those exhibited by other children targeted by coercive control. Within chapter 13 of her memoir, Buiso writes, "Evan's drinking only escalated. I pleaded with the powers that be at Juvenile Court to get him some help because he was constantly being written up for violating his probation by drinking. My son was not a criminal; he was a child with an illness that nobody wanted to treat. As Evan's drinking resumed, I was once again out looking for him in the dead of the night, terrified that I might find him dead by the side of the road."

Last winter, a mother contacted me, fearing for her child's life. Her teenage daughter "was cutting a lot," this mother reported to me. Her daughter also spoke of being "severely depressed." Her child was being forced to live primarily with the father, a man who had been an allegedly abusive husband during their marriage. The husband's history of spousal abuse did not cause alarm during the family court proceedings, this mother stated with exasperation.

"He is doing to her what he used to do to me. He times her with his watch. He took her bedroom door off of her room and took away all of her clothes. He then times her as she gets ready for school. When her father yells 'Go,' she has to run out of her room and find where in her father's house her clothes are hidden. Then, she has to get dressed within that pre-determined time frame. When the timer goes off, her father drags her out of the house and takes her to school in whatever state she is in. He used to do that to me, too. Time me. She is a teenager. She is just 16 years old. She is concerned about her appearance. She has become sullen and depressed and does not want to live with her father, but no one will believe us. And, there is more too. That's not the worst of it. No one will believe he is abusing her the way he used to abuse me. What can I do? I am afraid she is going to take her own life in order to escape this nightmare. What if she takes her own life when she's with him? What if I can't protect her?"

I had no answer. Through my networking and research, I knew the odds were stacked against such nurturing mothers and the children they tried to protect. This mother was desperate; I could feel her fear through the phone as she spoke. Her concerns made me think of a protective mother from The Netherlands who turned child-safety advocate and was maintaining a list of all the teenagers and children taken from their primary caregiver who have taken their lives as a result. Hundreds of names have been documented, and she kept those names on file. At my last review, her list contained approximately 500 to 600 names.

I wanted to find an answer for this mother, but I had nothing — nothing but validation that her experience was all too common and the recommendation to offer her concerns up in prayer as she had truly exhausted all legal avenues. She continued, "If all I had was money. Money is what I need in order to hire a good lawyer to help us both. But I have none. I feel all alone and desperate. My family won't help me."

Her words stung with truth. I have heard those words before.

This mother continued her desperate plea for help, stating, that if only she had the funds to afford legal representation, she could save her daughter's life. My heart sank once again. Money is not always the answer. A lawyer can claim to be in your corner, but sometimes not even a well-intentioned attorney firmly planted in your corner will guarantee that the court will rule in the child's best interest. This mother was taking full responsibility for the outcome, but it was not her fault. Sadly, the process has some mothers convinced they are the cause of the problem when they are not. This "gas-lighting" —when perpetrators of abuse or professional misconduct turn the tables and make the victim feel as if they are crazy or making things up —simply put, is blame-shifting manipulation.

I experienced this phenomenon firsthand during our 2013 trial. Our attorney stated for the record that he was the "busiest he has ever been," and failed "to prepare for trial." Knowing this can happen makes it almost impossible to assure a protective mother. I know from personal experiences and from the mothers who have shared their stories with me that even if she begs, borrows, and steals — as the old saying goes — she will not be guaranteed to win her case. The mothers I know did not fare well when the father petitioned for sole parental rights. Statistically speaking, a majority of fathers who petition for sole custody are awarded sole custody, regardless of whether or not the father has a criminal record or substance abuse problem.

Lights will guide you home.
And ignite your bones.
I will try to fix you.

This protective mother's anguish reminded me of the fears I had for my own children. First of all, Matthew and Amber, by genetics, are predisposed to anxiety and depression. Close relatives on both sides of their family have been diagnosed with one or both. My former husband's uncle committed suicide during his early twenties. Since modern-day medicine places so much emphasis on family history, this mother's fear was a fear I knew all too well. What Western medicine fails to recognize, however, is a family history of traumas and abuse. Unrecognized equates to untreated. Untreated equates to placing young children at risk. This is why I have become a proponent of trauma-informed healthcare professionals. Pediatricians are the gate keepers of children's health. If their medical training does not include being trauma-informed, they can easily misdiagnose a child with ADD or behavioral issues such as being oppositional and defiant. A child is not being oppositional or defiant when they disclose they do not want to be abused or bullied.

That child wants to be validated, supported, and protected. What kind of a human would intervene and prevent a mother from protecting her child from abuse? That is a question we protective mothers have been forced to ask ourselves over and over again.

I will circle back to the research conducted in the mid-1990s by the Center for Disease Control and Kaiser Permanente which "discovered an exposure that dramatically increased the risk for seven out of ten of the leading causes of death in the United States. In high doses, it affects brain development, the immune system, hormonal systems, and even the way our DNA is read and transcribed. Folks who are exposed in very high doses have a 20-year difference in life expectancy." That exposure is known as "childhood trauma," as stated by pediatrician Nadine Burke Harris, who describes such trauma as, "threats that are so severe or pervasive, such as growing up with substance dependence" — or fear. She included children growing up in constant fear of their personal safety. That was something I could relate to, given my stepfather's volatile temper and habit of walking into the bathroom or my bedroom while I was in the middle of disrobing. I understand what surviving the childhood home feels like. I understand what living in constant fear feels like. I was affected for years after I moved out of my childhood home. I locked the bathroom door wherever I went. As an adult, if I could to enter a bathroom, not lock the door, and feel a sense of safety, it was liberating.

According to the CDC's Adverse Childhood Experience research, even when children choose life over death, they are still at risk. Health risks include cancer or heart disease. The research affirms what loving, nurturing mothers know: It is not natural to be court-ordered out of a child's life. Intuitively, we mothers have always known how harmful it is for a child to be taken from us. We understand the risk of permanent health issues for the child. What we never considered was the risk to our own health. Instead, we discovered our own health issues after being court-ordered out of our children's lives. Some of the mothers I have spoken with suffer from complex PTSD and cannot hold down a full-time job. Maternal deprivation permanently affects the health of a mother, and primary care physicians should also be trauma-informed for this very reason.

According to Dr. Harris, "The Adverse Childhood Research Study is something everyone should know about." However, few medical doctors are trained to screen for adverse childhood experiences. Therefore, too many children are misdiagnosed with ADD or ADHD. She uses an analogy regarding well water that makes people sick. She stated you can either prescribe antibiotic after antibiotic, or you can provide clean water to the users of the well.

I understood her analogy about addressing the symptom or the actual problem first. I remember clearly my thoughts regarding my daughter's natural response to being removed from our family home and wanting to be returned to it. *Why don't they just let her come back to live with me? I do not understand how they cannot connect the dots. Her behaviors and medical symptoms all began within months of being taken out of our home.* Adding insult to injury, all of the symptoms and behaviors that were being used to frame my daughter as something she was not were normal reactions to an abnormal situation. She was not oppositional; she was traumatized. She was not lazy and irresponsible; she wanted to live with her primary attachment figure. She was not learning-disabled; she was exhibiting signs of chronic exposure to toxic stress. *How could no one else understand this? How is it that social workers were placed in the father's home?* The answer I kept getting: "To help him learn 'how' to parent properly."

When one state-mandated intervention did not work, another higher level of intervention was recommended. At one point, there was a social worker in the home two to three days each week, a case manager and a social worker to help support dad in learning how to organize and schedule after school activities that would permit Amber to be social. If I did not live this hellish nightmare, I would not believe it. For the first 15 years of my children's lives, I was able to coordinate after school and summer activities. Our children had been enrolled in several sports and child-appropriate activities such as Girl Scouts, dance classes, and T-ball. *Why on Earth would you take children out of a home that was child-centered and capable of placing the child's needs first and place them into a home in which the parent chose to work all the time, leaving the kids alone and isolated from their peers? Did the social workers not understand that isolation is* a form of control? I have come to recognize that if you isolate a human long enough, the human will trauma-bond with their captor. It is commonly referred to as Stockholm syndrome. Adults and children are prone to trauma-bonding. My educated guess is that children who are being isolated and controlled by the dominant parent will be at risk of creating a stronger bond with that parent than the nurturing one. The controlling parent's love is conditional, and those conditions lead a child to operate in survival mode. The child learns to protect, lie for, and attach to the parent who feeds them, buys them cell phones and cars, and determines their level of social isolation. The protective parent's love is unconditional. However, since the nurturing parent does not inflict negative consequences on the child if that loving bond is broken, perhaps children do not realize that losing that connection will only result in more intense isolation. The act of such maternal deprivation leads to the children not knowing their entire extended family, and these family members in turn are secondary victims of coercive control.

That said, I cannot fault a child wanting to survive their childhood household. Survival is a primitive instinct that is necessary for life. In the most rational way, I would rather my child choose life. If that meant letting go of the mother-child bond, then I had to let it go. Our healing and the restoration of our family unit was to be on their terms, not mine. Letting them go and allowing them to discover their truths and recognize the untruths told to them on their own time table has been the most difficult thing I have ever had to do. However, there is a silver lining; as of this writing, both of my children have chosen life. For a mother who loves her children unconditionally, there is consolation in this. For mothers who intuitively attempted to fix their child's every struggle and heartbreak, stepping back and allowing that child to live the natural consequences of their life choices takes exceptional strength and resolution.

The love and light within a mother's heart will guide her children back home someday, but we must be reminded that it is not our responsibility to "fix" any human, not even our own flesh and blood. In order for our children to fully evolve as humans and to fully mature as adults, they need to learn how to heal their own childhood wounds. We all have such wounds, and we have managed to survive. I have faith and trust that Matthew and Amber would continue their journey toward self-actualization. They, too, will survive. My parenting style was not that uncommon. I never wanted to over-step my boundary as a mother and mold them into what I wanted them to be. All I ever wanted to do was ensure that they knew of my unconditional love, and that my expectation was they would grow up to be compassionate and loving humans. I did not want them to become an extension of their father's self-serving behavior or emotionally abusive behaviors toward me. I kept reminding the children of my unconditional love, and that they always had another home to come home to.

> *When you try your best,*
> *But you don't succeed.*
> *When you get what you want,*
> *But not what you need.*
> *When you feel so tired,*
> *But you can't sleep...*
> *Stuck in reverse.*

My experience has taught me the only way to move out of reverse is to stop trying to fix people who do not want to be fixed. To provide my children with a path to return to our home, I had to let them go. I tried my best. I fought my hardest fight, given my financial constraints. I got my freedom. I got my life back, but I did not get the pleasure of being in my children's lives as they transitioned out of high school and entered into college. When you tire of worry and of being used as a target of coercive control, the only way to move forward is to let go of what no longer supports your highest good. I love my children, but I have to love and respect me, too, in a selfless way. Protective mothers, if you want your grown children to love and respect you, you need to love and respect yourself first. Love and light will guide your children home.

Chapter 6
Live Without Regrets

My best friend gave me the best advice.
He said each day's a gift and not a given right.
Leave no stone unturned, leave your fears behind.
And try to take the path less traveled by.
That first step you take is the longest stride.
~ Nickelback, "If Today Was Your Last Day."

Ever since I was a young child, I promised myself two things. The first was that I would never sacrifice myself for another human being. The second was twofold: I would do my best to live a life that I would be proud of, and I would not have regrets when I reflected upon my life choices. Throughout my life, I would occasionally question the commitments I had made to myself. One such example was when I became a mother. The immediate loving bond created from the birth of a child brought forth a commitment to do everything in my power to protect my child. I soon chose to give up relationships in order to protect my child. I would, in essence, sacrifice myself for my child. No doubt there were times when the two promises would morph just a little bit, but my resolve was always the same. I had made the commitment to be true to the woman I aspired to be, not in a self-serving way but instead in a self-preserving way. My childhood memories were of good times, but some memories were of fear and grounded in survival. As a child, I promised myself that when I was an adult, I would neither lie to protect another's poor choices nor would I sacrifice myself to build someone else up. If I am totally transparent and honest, there were times I did not live up to those commitments. Or, better stated, there were times when I failed. However, resiliency comes from the ability to reframe perceived failures as opportunities and perceived self-criticism as the chance to practice self-compassion. All of these factors circled back to my resolve to choose happiness and authenticity as my guiding light.

After my divorce, I was full of guilt and self-loathing. I remembered well the discomfort of being the child of a broken marriage. As a young adult, I had vowed to never end a marriage. For this very reason, it took two years from the day when I wrote a letter to Ned — stating I did not want to divorce but feared our marriage was falling apart — to my actually filing for our divorce. In those two years, he was too busy with work, and I was too busy caring for the home and our children and giving of myself as a community volunteer. The emotional disconnect from each other led to the natural consequence of our marital relationship becoming more and more strained. A year had passed, and the letter still sat in my husband's top drawer. I saw the letter every time I put away his laundry. There the letter stayed, and we had no conversation about it. I was too afraid to say something out loud. My fear was that if I spoke of this letter, I would open the door to conflict. Conflict would lead to the children overhearing an argument. I believed Ned ignored the letter and avoided the topic hoping that I was too dependent on him for financial support to actually leave the marriage; I now understand that Ned was probably afraid to broach the topic of our failing marriage.

After a year had passed by, I knew that if our marriage was to succeed, I had to be the one to ensure that it happened. I confided in a friend who had recently been to marriage counseling and asked her for the name of her counselor. Ned and I met with the same counselor. Another year would pass. Counseling for us did not restore our relationship. I knew that to remain in a marriage that was no longer founded in a partnership was to turn our relationship into my in-laws' marriage. At first glance, my mother-in-law appeared to be comfortable with her role as her husband's servant, but she was anxious and nervous all the time. She did not seem authentically happy. Undoubtedly, my mother-in-law loved her children and grandchildren. She was most joyful when she was in their presence. But it was clear her own marriage was strained. I did not want to be that kind of person, a person who goes through the motions of life, who just exists.

I initiated our divorce in the latter part of 2005. The act of terminating our marriage spurred a long-term commitment to reexamine my life yet again in order to take responsibility for what I perceived as my failures. The only way to a life of joy and happiness was to own what part I took in my own sorrow and sense of guilt. An examined life leads to the awareness to make different choices. I had no one to blame but me. Or so I thought. I now realize that a marriage requires the commitment of two people. One person alone cannot carry the entire burden of a marriage's success.

From working to become more responsible for me and for others — specifically, for our children — I grew to be more and more reflective. I learned to check in with myself often and to examine my thoughts, my actions, and my choices. I was far from perfect and completely human, but I never blamed others for my shortcomings or for struggles. I learned to put a name to my feelings and permitted myself to feel them. Facing my own character flaws at times led me to one or two too many glasses of wine. Having done a lot of research on trauma and its effects, I was aware there was a danger in numbing my feelings.

I remember making a conscious decision to focus on my health. I knew that stress unmanaged could lead to several health problems. Our family had members who struggled with food addiction, drug and alcohol addition, and a propensity to use gambling and lottery games to avoid the feelings that go along with the sense that we somehow failed in life. I no longer stood in judgment of others once I understood what this emotional pain felt like, the kind of deep-down pain that is associated with the knowledge that you let your own children down: the knowledge that they, too, had to deal with the challenges that are associated with living between two separate households.

I concluded that it is one thing to let your parents down. Heck, I was used to doing that. I also understood how it must have felt like to let my husband down. He was divorced once before, and now he had to deal with his own sense of failure having divorced a second time. I let myself down. I was responsible for that and I owned it. But to let your children down is the kind of pain that is difficult to describe unless you have been there.

"If today was your last day and tomorrow was too late, could you say goodbye to yesterday? Would you live each moment like your last? Leave old pictures in the past? Donate every dime you had, if today was your last day?"

If I had made a commitment to myself that was relatively easy to follow, then now was the time to make a similar commitment to my children. I was hurting deep into my soul, knowing that I had been responsible for the hurt Matthew and Amber felt when I divorced their father. Reminding myself of the statistic that one in two marriages ends in divorce did not make me feel any better. Having my former husband reminding me how hard life was for him after our divorce did not boost my sense of being able to make good choices either. No one, other than my pastor, knew how crushed I was when my marriage dissolved. I told no one how devastated I was. I felt guilty for feeling guilty.

I knew I was falling down a rabbit hole, so I opted to reframe and recommit to myself and to my children. I would fight like hell to live each and every day making the best decisions to ensure a happy future for the three of us. In hindsight, I now understand how I set myself up for failure. I now know, 11 years later, I am not responsible for anyone else's happiness. We parents try — and for good reason — to create a perfect and happy childhood for our children, but that is not possible. Parents are human. Parents make a lot of mistakes. The question is this: Can we forgive ourselves for our mistakes? If so, then we certainly can forgive others for their mistakes.

I kept up the habit of self-reflection and the resolve to always do better tomorrow. I learned to live each day as if it were my last. This resolve was the catalyst for planning the 2010 vacation with Matthew and Amber. Unbeknownst to them, their father had served me with court papers four months prior. He sought residential custody of Matthew five days a week and Amber three. Like a mother tiger protecting her cubs, I fought the court motion with everything I had. But I felt as if I was losing. My maternal intuition had me sensing that if Ned had the financial support of his family, he could out-lawyer me. I had been living check-to-check and slowly draining my savings. The financial burden of paying upwards of

$200 per hour for a lawyer as well as a court-appointed, guardian ad litem took a financial toll on me. What if Ned won residential custody because he could afford a nicer home than me? What if I became so poor that I could no longer provide for my children? My mother was living out of state, as were my siblings. I had nowhere to go, no one to move in with. And no one to turn to. My family was not a family of great financial means. At a time when I should have been scraping my pennies together, I chose to take my tax return and splurge on a family vacation. As of this writing, it remains the last family vacation my children and I had.

If I was to lose being their primary caregiver, I wanted us to have the memory of the three of us having no cares or concerns, even if it was just for five days. In truth, the few thousand dollars it took to create memories that last a lifetime would not have prevented me from losing our family home in the fall of 2010. Ned had been advised by his lawyer to stop paying court-ordered child support about two months after we returned from our family vacation. Three months of no child support led to the inability to pay our mortgage. That led to foreclosure notices being mailed to our home. I was at the end of my rope, desperate, unable to think coherently. I panicked. How would I provide for the children? How would the move from a $500,000 home to a small, two-bedroom condo to — potentially — a homeless shelter impact the children? What do they need? They need a parent who can provide for them, right? So, without realizing what coercive control was, what financial abuse was, or how the court process could financially disable a mother, I gave in to my lawyer's advice: Quit.

"My advice for you is to give up," she told me. "Sign whatever it is that they put before us. I can keep fighting for you, and I can spend more of your money, but I guarantee you that we are going to lose."

I was in complete disbelief. How on earth can a lawyer predict the outcome? Was it not up to the judge to determine the outcome? Or me? What about me wanting to provide for my own family? Was that too much to ask, to be left alone and no longer harassed or scrutinized or forced into poverty? My head spun. My heart sank. My stomach sickened at the thought that I had to do the unthinkable: I signed the new agreement, which afforded Ned legal residential custody of both children while maintaining joint custody for decision-making.

In order to put the children's needs before my own, I sacrificed my need to have them in my home. At that time, August of 2010, I knew nothing of the ACE research. I knew nothing about the Saunders study. I knew nothing about trauma and the effects of trauma. I knew nothing about the signs of trauma. I had broken my promise to myself to always put my wellbeing first. From having no knowledge of how devastating it is for children to be taken away from their primary caregiver, I truly thought their father could provide better. I truly thought money was happiness. What I have since learned is that money can make life easier and less challenging, but access to money does not guarantee happiness, and having access to money does not replace a loving mother's nurturing.

I immediately felt trapped, betrayed, and desperate. I was able to find a tenant for my condo. Their rent paid for my mortgage, and that kept me from going into foreclosure. I then sold off everything I had that had any value. I did everything in my power to pay down debt and to provide for my children without them ever feeling as if we were poor or they were a burden. I held two jobs. I worked fulltime, Monday through Friday, and then worked part-time on Saturday mornings. I may not be rich, I told myself, but I am a fighter and a survivor. I may not be able to buy my children fancy gadgets or luxuries, but I can model for my kids what resilience looks like. I am sure neither child was aware of how dire my financial situation was. I did not lie to the children; I just chose not to weigh them down with burdens that were not theirs to carry.

A year or two later, Amber was given an opportunity to travel out of the country with her school classmates. The trip was as expensive as the family trip we had taken in 2010. However, Amber was selected for this opportunity because of her good grades, civic involvement within her school, and for being a highly responsible seventh-grader. She wanted to go, and I wanted to provide for her opportunities that were never given to me. We made the commitment to solicit support from family and friends, and lo and behold, Amber was able to go.

I wanted the children to learn how to be resourceful as well as resilient. I wanted the children to never feel as if they had to sacrifice life opportunities just because their parents had divorced. I wanted to model for the children the fine line between stock piling money while never venturing out beyond work and home and making thoughtful choices regarding opportunities that may pass you by if not taken when they are presented. Work hard? Yes. Save for a rainy day? Yes. But do not postpone life until you are of retirement age hoping that you have the health to support travel and once-in-a-life-time adventures. Life is too short to not live. Life is too short to not seek opportunity and joy.

If today was your last day would you make your mark by mending a broken heart? You know it is never too late to shoot for the stars. Regardless of who you are. So do whatever it takes 'Cause you can't rewind a moment in your life. Let nothing stand in your way.

Forgiveness and grace are gifts — gifts to both receive and to give. For years, I vacillated between wanting to track down my biological father and imagining the pain that reuniting with my biological father might bring my mother. It was quite clear that the topic of my father caused her emotional distress. She had wounds that she never took the time to heal. That is the funny thing about emotional wounds. You can bury them, deny them, avoid them, and convince yourself you have moved on from them, but in truth, they rear their ugly heads when you least expect it. I never understood how deep the wound of not having my father in my life was for me.

The story goes that he left my mother when I was not quite two years old. I have a black-and- white photo of him holding me on his lap, but I have no memory of him. In theory, I never knew him, so how could his loss wound me? Maybe that answer was the shame and the stigma that is connected to not knowing your biological father. "I was fine," I would often try to convince myself. "I don't need someone who did not need me," I would rationalize. However, when my sister and I finally found the courage to search for our father, we discovered he had died in 2009. I felt sucker-punched that I let myself down yet again. I had thought of trying to find him in the early 1990s, but I was convinced I was too broke to take on the expense of a private detective. In hindsight, I now wonder if I made the right decision. The finality of a person being gone from this planet pained my heart. But it was not until I visited Ms. Buiso, who coincidently lived within 20 minutes of where my father had been buried, that I understood how deep a person can bury a childhood wound. It was the fall of 2016; seven years after his death, I sat on the ground by his headstone. From deep down within me, I released a guttural wail. I spoke with him. I told him I loved him, even though I never knew him. I forgave him for not being there for our family. I trusted he did the best he could, given the challenges he faced. As a mother, I knew how hard it was to choose what you think is best for your children.

If I could forgive him for his complete absence, was it possible that Matthew and Amber would someday forgive me for signing the 2010 divorce agreement? I hoped so. I never intended to make the children feel abandoned — an adjective Ned used over and over and over again whenever he had an opportunity to email me. I truly believe that one cannot ask for grace without being willing to offer it. One cannot ask for forgiveness without being able to forgive. Once cannot judge another without the risk of being judged in return. These were some of the hardest lessons to learn. Forgiveness and grace are gifts to be given as well as gifts to be received.

Let nothing
Stand in your way,
'Cause the hands of time
Are never on your side.

Let nothing stand in the way of protecting your children; live a life of no regrets. Protective mothers, do whatever you have to do to keep your children safe. This portion of my memoir is dedicated to a protective mother who lived those very words. Her name is Shannon Baskin. I met her through social media networking, and we soon became friends online. Her story is jaw-dropping. She was a fervent social justice advocate, and she let nothing stand in her way when it came to being reunited with her children. According to a December

14, 2017, post online, Shannon was quoted as saying, "The shock of losing my child to a man she has no blood or legal ties to and is my ex-abuser almost killed me." Baskin had lost custody of her teenage daughter to a former boyfriend — not a former husband but a boyfriend who was not the teenager's father.

The case summary written by The Women's Coalition (TWC) states, "In 2015, Shannon lost custody of her three children to her ex-boyfriend, who is the father of her two younger sons but not the older daughter. Judge David Roper disregarded facts and evidence which showed Shannon was the better parent: a domestic violence conviction; DUIs; Shannon was the primary nurturer; the daughter hardly knew him." The post went on to state that the judge put a "gag order" on Shannon to "keep her from exposing his bias and corruption." Included within the post was a link to 2015 local news coverage by Fox 54, "Family Court Investigation, Local Woman Filing Suit Against Judge." I had watched the news coverage a few years prior when Shannon was online trying to warn others about family court bias. I witnessed the tenacious fight Shannon gave to have her daughter returned to her care. I was horrified that a child could be court-ordered to live with someone who was not a parent. I was equally shocked to hear of Shannon's untimely death in 2017. TWC's post stated, "Shannon passed away in her sleep the night before last. The cause of death unknown. She had regained custody of her daughter in August but not her sons." I had to agree with TWC's statement that Shannon was "a hero for fighting so hard to keep and protect her children." Weeks after the online post, a friend of mine located the medical examiner's report. It was concluded that her untimely death was a result of an accidental over-dose. I wonder if she was prescribed medications to address psychic shock. Psychic shock — a state of physical shock — is a term often used by abuse survivor Coral Anika Theil. Or, did Shannon have a high ACE score? We will never know.

High levels of toxic stress are literally killing protective mothers and children targeted by coercive control. Shannon — not unlike Susan B. Anthony or Joan of Arc — fought for justice. Shannon was a tenacious advocate for women and children. I hope her family and friends are proud of her. Live life without regrets. Our children deserve no less. In Shannon's memory, this chapter is dedicated to her.

The universe is not trying to break you, my dear, it's trying to find a way to wake you up so that you see what is real and worth fighting for. It takes time to heal, but it also takes courage.

~Author Unknown

Chapter 7
Speaking Truth To Power

*Oh, what I would do to have the kind of strength it takes
to stand before a giant with a sling and a stone, surrounded
by the sound of a thousand warriors shaking in their armor,
wishing they'd have had the strength to stand, But the giant's
calling out my name, and he laughs at me, reminding me of
all the times I tried and failed.*
~Casting Crowns, *"Voice of Truth."*

I have procrastinated with the writing of this memoir for a few
years now. The timing was never quite right. Over time, however, I
have learned to trust my instincts. I now laugh to myself that the
original title for this memoir was going to be *The View from Under
The Bus*. Anyone who has had any experience exposing an injustice
or a perpetrator of abuse will be familiar with the terms victim-
blaming, victim-shaming, smear campaign, and gas-lighting. But as
they say, "timing is everything." When I first realized that writing a
memoir would be cathartic, I was not healed enough to take on such
a project. I was still in the throes of fighting for my own life and for
the lives of my children.

Matthew and Amber had no idea what was going on behind the
scenes, and at the same time, I truly had no idea what their home life
was like. We would get together as a family and talk about anything
else but their home life. I noticed that over time that Amber opened
up less and became more closed off emotionally. Prior to the January
2014 trial outcome, she would confide in me all the time. The
following year, she texted me asking when she could move back in
with me. Her asking to move back into my home was something she
had done a half-dozen times or more prior to the trial outcome. Even
though I was emotionally exhausted from all of the prior court
filings, I could not say "no" to Amber's 2015 request. I knew she
wanted back into our home, and I knew I was more than capable of
providing her a home environment that would allow her to heal from

the trauma that was a byproduct of systemic failures to protect her from chronic stress. She and I together fought one last fight, petitioning the court to permit her to move back into my home her final year of high school, but the court petition was denied.

We waited until the end of her junior year of high school, hoping the court would view her request as a clean start for her senior year. At first, the court was open to the idea. The magistrate ordered Ned to allow Amber to spend two-thirds of the summer vacation under my care. The magistrate made the mistake, however, of leaving that arrangement for Ned to organize and comply with on his own. The plan per the magistrate's court order was for us to follow up at the end of the summer to assess Amber's acclimation to my new home, which by that time included my present husband. Her mistake was to assume that Ned would follow through with the court order. Ned did not. So, by the time we were invited back to family court to discuss how Amber adjusted to my home, we had nothing to report. At this point, the magistrate was equally frustrated. The magistrate gave up and dismissed the petition. It is important to note that no sanctions were made against Ned for not following court the order.

In hindsight, I think that was the final straw for Amber. She became sullen and withdrawn. It was now the fall of 2015, and she had tried in vain for five years to speak her truth to power. But no one but me listened. Amber's senior year was spent at a high school full of students and professionals that never understood her cries for help.

Amber's behavior reminds me of a story of an African-American man sent to prison for a crime he did not commit. He was sent to prison for life even though he was innocent. This prisoner stated that after years of trying to have his sentence over-turned due to his innocence, he decided to just stop talking. He would not say "hello" or "good bye" to fellow inmates. And if a prison guard asked him a question, he wrote his answer on a piece of paper. The innocent man stated, "When you speak your truths for years and no one listens, you get to a point in which you just do not want to talk anymore." I think something similar happened to Amber during that summer. She had been kept from me rather than being allowed to spend the summer with me. That isolation for all of her summer vacation was the final straw for her.

For reasons unknown to me, Amber backed out of going to her senior prom at the last minute and opted not to participate in her high school graduation ceremonies. It was extremely painful as a mother to be forced to sit back and watch a beautiful, vibrant, intelligent young woman retreat within, becoming a ghost of someone who was once labeled as a gifted and talented student. She spoke truth to power, and she lost. Her voice taken, her actions resembled someone hopeless and robotic. This was not the daughter I raised. I had to step back and permit her to succumb to her environment. The older she got, the less I was able to protect her. The older she got, the more beaten down she had become: disempowered and hopeless.

As I sit here in my home office, writing on the first day of 2018, I begin to reflect upon the global social justice accomplishments of the last year. It was the year of the first international, Women's March, and — 2017 was also the year to lift up those who spoke out. As a follow-up to the #metoo campaign, TIME Magazine published as a cover feature the well-known 2017 women dubbed the "Silence-Breakers." The powerful began exposing the powerful: Hollywood women began a global violence-against-women awareness campaign, outing well-known and often previously well-liked perpetrators of sexual harassment and assault.

During the same year when I finally committed to writing my memoir, TIME Magazine's Person of the Year award honored more silence-breakers. These women included Ashley Judd, Susan Fowler, Adama Iwu, and Taylor Swift. "The galvanizing actions have unleashed one of the high-velocity shifts in our culture since the 1960s. Social media acted as a powerful accelerant," the article states, going on to acknowledge the "floodgates" are now open. For me, the #metoo campaign dovetails with the domestic abuse-awareness #nomore. Couple the #nomore success with that of the 2017 Women's March, and I truly believe our Protective Mothers Movement is soon to follow. I have no doubt that 2018 will be the year that we women will be heard. I have no doubt that the vision I had for this memoir will be far better supported in this new year.

If I had published a few years ago, I risked no one taking notice because the subject matter would have been deemed too unbelievable. Truth be told, there have been hundreds and hundreds of silence-breakers prior to 2017. I refer to these women as the pioneers of social justice and trailblazers for the Protective Mothers Movement of 2018. One shining example is an author and advocate by the name of Coral Anika Theill. Her social media page contains this quote: "The woman you are becoming will cost you people, relationships, spaces, and material things. Choose her over everything." I consider Coral a part of my tribe, a friend, a support person, and a mentor. She published her memoir *BONSHEA: Making Light of the Dark* in 2003, with a revision in 2013. Coral maintains a web site at www.coralanikatheill.com devoted to supporting people through their trauma recovery. Although Coral and I have never met in person, we have shared experiences that have positioned us on the same spiritual path of being agents of change. We are not alone. As Donna Buiso, who had published her memoir in 2016, shared with me on more than one occasion, to speak truth to power is to risk a backlash.

I am well aware of smear campaigns. As a result of speaking truth to power, I have been a target of more than one. I have hinted earlier of an experience I had involving a faith leader. When I exposed him as a perpetrator of professional misconduct, I was targeted almost immediately. I wrote a short synopsis of my experience with spiritual abuse, and that summary is contained within The Hope of Survivors website. After exposing my former pastor's professional misconduct, I went on with my life, using the same strategies for healing I had used in the past: counseling, reflection, taking responsibility for my part of my human frailties, and learning not to own what was not my cross to bear. Victims of any form of abuse are not to be blamed; however, I could learn how to protect myself better as I moved forward with my resolve to choose more healthy relationships. Paying attention to red flags is one useful strategy. I put my present husband — God bless his soul — under more scrutiny than I imagined possible. We joke about how he is "tougher than the rest." And, he is. I had to be tough. After all, I had been abused by the three most influential men in my life: my stepfather, faith leader, and first husband. It is a wonder that I learned to trust again. With God's grace, a lot of counseling, and a lot of personal commitment to heal my trauma, I did learn to trust again.

For me, writing is both painful and healing. I wrote for The Hope of Survivors and was invited to participate in the writing of the book *Deception in the Pews: Exposing the hidden dangers lurking within religions*. I attended one of the annual national conferences held in Washington, D.C., and coordinated by the Survivors Network of those Abused by Priests. This organization is commonly referred to by the acronym SNAP. It was there that I met activist and abuse survivor Angela Shelton for the second time and there that I met attorney and author Wendy Murphy who was selling her newly published book *And Justice For Some*. Fascinated by law, I purchased her book and read it, hoping to better understand the failures of our American justice system from the perspective of a lawyer.

As I look back and reflect, two things come to mind that appear to me as foreshadowing. One was a reference the last page of her book made to family court. Her book was focused on civil court cases, the types of cases that are popular in made-for-TV viewing. To paraphrase, her perspective was, "Don't get me going on what happens in family court." I remember thinking, "What? What goes on in family court?" The year was 2008, I believe. I was two years divorced by that time, and other than the feelings of shame, guilt, and failure, my experience with family court was uneventful. I had no idea what was coming with the end of 2009.

The second thing I found serendipitous was that Wendy Murphy became the attorney for Kelly Rutherford the *Gossip Girl* alum, in that very same year. According to a December 16, 2015, *US Magazine* article, Rutherford lost custody of her eight and six-year-old children. "According to *Daily Mail*, a Monaco judge awarded Giersch her former husband full custody of their children. Hermes and Helena will continue to live with the German businessman in Monaco. They will no longer be allowed to visit Rutherford in the U.S., and the star will only be able to visit them in France or Monaco," the article states, noting the actress had to file bankruptcy after spending "nearly $1.5 million on legal fees" This is the protective mothers conundrum: We do not have the money to spend on exorbitant legal fees. When a protective mother gives into the unrelenting pressure of coercive control, she is forced to choose between bankruptcy and being deprived of involvement in the lives of her own children.

For me, this conundrum is the epitome of the proverbial war on women: Being deprived of the mother-and-child relationship is the absolute worst form of abuse any human could inflict on another. My hope is that the Protective Mothers Movement will bring this atrocity to light and the federal government will enact accountability and oversight for the state procedures that are ultimately responsible for maternal deprivation. A father may initiate the court process, but ultimately it is the actions and inactions of the courts that position children in an unsafe environment. This is why organizations are pleading with the American public: Without your activism, thousands and thousands more American children will be placed in jeopardy.

Oh what I would do to have the kind of faith it takes to climb out of this boat I'm in onto the crashing waves, To step out of my comfort zone into the realm of the unknown where Jesus is and he's holding out his hand, But the waves are calling out my name and they laugh at me reminding me of all the times I've tried and failed, the waves keep telling me time and time again, "boy, you'll never win!" But the voice of truth tells me another story...

Smear campaigns. As a person who chooses to speak truth to power, be prepared for the eventual smear campaign. To date, I have been the target of three of them. As a child, my step-father framed me as the troublemaker. I was labeled the black sheep of the family. I clearly remember being told "not to make waves" by my mother. I remember being told again by my mother to "be nice" to my stepfather. As a child, I vacillated between being bold and standing up for myself and wanting to please my stepfather in order to keep peace within the family and bridge some form of alliance with him in the hopes that the abuse would not escalate. I knew there was a possibility I would be raped; it was common knowledge that young girls were often victimized by stepfathers like him. I clearly remember thinking that if I bought him nice presents for Christmas,

Father's Day, and his birthday, maybe he would be less apt to cross the line from voyeurism to sexual assault.

As I reflect on those experiences, I understand why children keep quiet about familial abuse. I knew even then that if I spoke up about the maltreatment and no one believed me, there was a good chance the abuse would begin escalating, and that was something I was not prepared to risk. As an adult looking back, I am beside myself thinking of how many of us well-meaning adults position children into being their own silence-breaker, only to have the same children face a system set up to dismiss their disclosures. More than 30 years later, I was forced to sit back with my hands tied and watch my daughter be targeted while no one believed her. I was framed as the emotionally abusive one coaching her to dislike her father, and she was framed as being oppositional or unstable. Amber and I tried to speak truth to power, and we were ignored. And in the end, we were the target of a smear campaign.

Then, later, as a parishioner groomed for professional misconduct by my faith leader, I was framed as a woman scorned by the man who had taken advantage of me. It was almost comical because once I discovered his lies and deception, the last thing I wanted was to have our relationship resume. I was not a woman scorned. I was a woman who had taught a child- empowerment program that was founded on the beliefs that no one has the right to abuse you; if someone chooses to abuse you, it is not your fault; and since it is not your fault, you need to keep telling your story until someone believes you and protects you. As an adult who taught these lessons to hundreds of children, how could I silently slink away and hope this pastor did not prey on another parishioner? I felt compelled to expose the truths, even though it meant placing my private life under scrutiny and putting myself in a position to be victimized by those who chose to believe their pastor could do no wrong. I had no idea that he and his small group of enablers would choose to write anonymous letters to my workplace stating I should be fired. They even went so far as to spread the lie that I was diagnosed as bipolar. I mean no disrespect for those who have a mental health diagnosis. My issue is with the fact that it was a lie and was being spread all over the town in which my young children attended school. My former pastor and his cohorts were harming my children by destroying my reputation. I knew nothing about narcissism back then. However, I am now fully aware of the term and the behaviors associated with a sociopathic narcissist. Those plagued by the disorder often project onto the victim their own character flaws. And if you expose them, they often resort to smear campaigns and do whatever they can to shift the blame and try to make others forget. Their favorite phrases for their victims? Quite often, they include, "move on," and "get over it."

It was my family physician who informed me that our pastor was telling his deacons to spread the rumor that I was bipolar and, therefore, not to be believed. I was at a medical appointment when this doctor quietly asked permission to take off the doctor hat and put on a community-member hat.

"Sure," I said. I was curious as to what was to follow.

"I thought you would want to know that James Kimball, the head deacon, is telling everyone that you are bipolar. He got into a conversation with my spouse and said that you were not to be believed because you are bipolar. My spouse does not know that you are my patient. I cannot tell anyone that you are my patient because of your right to privacy. But, I thought you should know about the rumors they are spreading about you all over town."

"Thank you for being honest with me. I am not surprised. Do you know that anonymous letters had been sent to my home as well as to my workplace? They were threatening in nature. I know they are meant to intimidate me, but I was prepared. Pastor Ralph threatened to retaliate against me when I broke up with him and told him that I did not want to speak with him ever again. I had two minor children to protect. I was not going to stay involved — not even in a platonic nature — with a man who knowingly used a newly divorced mother who was caring for two young children. He knew full well what his ethical obligations were. He knew full well about the imbalance of power, but he pursued me none-the-less. I cannot forgive a man who preys on the vulnerabilities of single mothers. It is unconscionable."

"I knew you did not have a mental health diagnosis, but I could not say anything to my spouse or to the parishioners of our church. My parents love that church. My family has attended that church forever. If it feels any better, know that there are many people who support you. Many others have come forward with their experiences with Pastor Ralph. But, the church deaconate like him. He is their buddy. They also feel bad about his kids. They do not want his ex-wife to be impoverished as a result of him no longer earning six figures a year. It's really complicated and a shame for all involved."

I remember leaving my doctor's office feeling at once victimized and empowered because my physician did not have to tell me what had happened and yet had supported me. From there, I was able to contact the deaconate and his wife and kindly asked them to stop spreading lies in regard to my mental health or a civil suit would soon follow. The rumor-mill stopped churning out its lies about me. I do recall, however, hearing that one of the individuals who had been spreading those lies soon took ill. In my heart of hearts, I do believe that there is a Higher Power working to support the truth. And, I also believe that when an opportunity for repentance presents itself and one chooses to cover up lies with more lies, then some form of negative karmic energy will soon follow. The truth came to light when within six months of my former pastor's next conquest, a Valentine's Day wedding was performed and in August they became parents to a healthy baby girl. The rumors about town then were all about the baby's "early arrival." I just thanked the good Lord above that I was spared any more time in a relationship with this man.

Looking back on that whole experience, I am left to wonder how is it that we as a society discount a victim's story of abuse based solely on the victim's past. In my situation, the diagnosis was made up in order to cast doubt on my truth-telling. But, in reality, a perpetrator is keen enough to target victims in their time of weakness. Sometimes the "weak" person may be a newly divorced and highly vulnerable mother. Other times, the "weak" one maybe a child who is living in an abusive home, a person who is homeless, a person who has just lost a job, a person grieving after having lost a parent, or a person struggling with a drug or alcohol addiction. Or, it may be a person truly struggling with a mental health diagnosis. How is it that we as a society judge whether or not a victim of abuse is telling the truth because of their past or present life situation?

This is why victims of abuse remain silent. The perpetrators carefully select someone who has something to lose if they disclose. In my personal situation, it was rumored that Pastor Ralph targeted professional women in troubled marriages or women who were newly divorced and used his pastoral counseling services as a way to romantically involve himself with them, all the while knowing that their professional lives would be put at risk if they were to disclose these indiscretions. I was the first parishioner in more than a decade to expose this pastor to his pastoral licensing organization. I was believed by the investigative committee, and as such, a letter of apology was sent to my home address. But what if I had tragedy or mistakes in my past? Or had a mental health disability? Or was addicted to drugs? Would I have been believed then? This is a question that will need more unpacking as the #metoo, #nomore, #ustoo, and #timesup campaigns move forward. How do we protect the most vulnerable? How do we encourage more people to speak truth to power and not have them become re-victimized in the process?

But the stone was the right size to put the giant on the ground and the waves they don't seem high from on top of them looking down, I will soar with the wings of eagles when I stop and listen to the sound of Jesus singing over me. I will choose to listen and believe the voice of truth.

Smear campaigns. I am used to them. I have stared them down, and I have survived them. Having had the prior experience, I feel as if I was not as wounded as I could have been when the paperwork submitted to the courts attempted to frame me as an unfit mother. They could never prove I was unfit. It was gossip at best and a legal strategy at worst. I am not sorry if my truths make another person uncomfortable or angry. It is not my job to protect the feelings of a perpetrator or the actions of those who choose misconduct over being ethical. In my own spiritual journey, I have had to make the decision over and over again: Do I want to do what is popular and make friends with those who live in denial? Or, do I speak my truths and risk alienation? Do I risk losing those people and relationships that Coral Anika Theil's social media page references? In the end, I chose the latter. I chose the truth over being popular and in relationships with people who were not authentic to me. Protective mothers, we need to model for our children what truth-telling looks like. Be a silence-breaker. Be a peaceful warrior. Be authentic. In the end, you will give your children the strength to choose the same.

I will choose to listen and believe the voice of truth.

Chapter 8
Lessons in Humility and Kindness

Hold the door, say please, say thank you
Don't steal, don't cheat, and don't lie
I know you got mountains to climb, but
Always stay humble and kind.
~Tim McGraw, *"Humble and Kind"*

My dear beloved Matthew, I want to see you be humble and kind.

"Childhood stars shine. Always stay humble and kind," are the lyrics within Tim McGraw's song, "Humble and Kind." Matthew, as of 2015, these lyrics made me think of you every time the song played on my radio. Several months ago, when the emotional wounds were still fresh, I would hear this song at work, and the tears would flow. Odd how a simple lyric, or word, or item such as a mountain bike would shift my thoughts straight back on you. My mind would then flood with memories. And questions, too: Why? Why can't we speak to each other? What words were spoken to you to prompt you to stop all contact with me? What could be so powerful that it changed you?

And, then, as a mother, I worry about you.

Are you really ok? Really? How is college? How is your training going? How can I help?

I miss you, son. I loved you before I met you. Despite what we have gone through as individuals and together, my love for you only deepens. Our distance — both emotional and physical — pains me. So many conversations have happened between you and me with only me participating: My mind's inner dialogue serving as a coping skill to remain sane when someone I love is unreachable. Since the summer of 2016, I have found solace by walking to the beach over one-hundred times, just to pray. I hoped the ocean breezes would transport my hugs and the whispered "I love yous" to you. I prayed that your guardian angels would hug you, for me, with their angel wings and bring you my love from miles away. I wonder, did you ever spontaneously feel my love? Did my prayers and meditation actually work?

I miss you, son. I look forward to the day when we can get to know each other again. It has been more than two years since we sat at a table together sharing a meal. It feels like an eternity. But that is from a mother's standpoint. I am told by experts and professionals that maybe our distance is not as traumatic for you, as the child because children are at that age of natural separation and, therefore, distracted by college and friends. I often pray that you are surrounded by abundance. Not wealth necessarily, but an abundance of good friends, love, support systems, good health, guardian angels, common sense, and good judgment. I also wish for you the gifts of humility and kindness.

I reflect back and admit that the days and dates get blurry. Was it June of 2015 or 2016 that I saw you last? Trauma and loss are so difficult to manage, but I found a way. It appears that you have found a way as well. That makes me so proud of you. I have always been proud of you. I was proud to accompany you on your first day at university. Remember how the wooden desk in your dorm room had your initials carved inside the desk drawer? Crazy, we thought! A previous student had your same initials. What are the chances? I remember thinking that it was a sign from above that you were meant to be there. As a mother, that thought gave me comfort. This was the start of your new journey as a young adult. I cherished sending you care packages and having the opportunity to visit you, on campus, four months later. Remember? Joseph and I took you to Olive Garden after the college hockey game. I felt so honored being in your presence and to have you as my son.

You probably do not remember much from your early childhood. Therefore, this entire chapter will be devoted to you: my memories of you and us. Should we never speak again, I wanted you to know something about my most cherished memories of you. My prayer is that will not be the case for us. Well, here are a few of my memories.

First of all, the simple act of reflection upon our time spent together brings a smile immediately to my face. I feel joy when I think of you. I am so very grateful for the time we did have together. Here, I choose to focus on our joys and on my gratitude. Son, you were meant to be born. Our story was meant to be told. My fight was meant to be fought. This book meant to be written. So, I thank you. I am grateful for the process because I am now a more empowered woman who feels compassion for every soul on this Earth. I am a better person simply because I gave birth to you.

You were born on a Wednesday. Funny, in applying for my present job, I had to search back to the actual day — not the date but the day — of my birth. I, too, was born on a Wednesday. As was your sister, 20 months after your birth. I can hear your sister's dry wit as I imagine her reacting to the fun fact that all three of us were born on Wednesdays: *"It's like we are related!"* Yes. You were born on a Wednesday in the heat of the summer. Instantly, I fell in love with you. The kind of love I experienced and still do is impossible to put into words, however. One has to experience it in order to understand. As a male, you will never experience childbirth firsthand, but if you choose to become a father, I hope you cherish the actual birth of your child and appreciate the miracle of birth. Lift up the mother of your child and honor her with the utmost respect. Son, I want to see you be humble and kind.

I have to admit that I may have been an over protective mother, but I was not an over bearing one. There is a difference. Your health and safety were, and still are, of utmost importance to me. Your needs were always addressed. As a matter of fact, when your sister was born, I had hired a mother's helper to watch over you when I was busy nursing your baby sister. Infants nurse often. I was too shy to nurse outdoors. You, however, lived to be outdoors. So the mother's helper was responsible for playing outdoors with you so that your needs were not neglected.

Your interactions with Amber when she first came home from the hospital were priceless. You would try to engage her in conversation. *"Hi. Hi. Hi. H,"* you repeated. You were so confused when she did not respond. You were only 20 months old. You were excited to have a baby sister, but not overly impressed with her inability to respond to your salutations. Little did you know then that your baby sister would grow up looking toward you for life direction. Amber would soon be your first best friend.

Your next closest best friend was your cousin Nathaniel. He was born four months after you. His mother, your aunt, was the person who brought your dad and me together. She set us up on a blind date. I fell madly in love with your dad. He was a great guy, I thought. Please know that despite all we have endured, I still do think well of your father. It is through several life lessons and from analytic meditation that I have learned compassion for all of the souls that walk this Earth. I share with you my new-found perspective for a several reasons. Long story short son is that I want you to grow and mature to learn the benefit of humility and kindness.

> *Don't expect a free ride from no one*
> *Don't hold a grudge or a chip and here's why*
> *Bitterness keeps you from flying*
> *Always stay humble and kind.*

I used to take some of the tings your father said and did so personally. By doing so, I got hurt. My feelings were hurt over, and over again. I can reflect back and state that his words and actions had nothing to do with me. His words and actions have nothing to do with you, either. I understand that your dad had his own fears and his own reasons for who he was then and is today. I cannot allow myself to be hurt or angry anymore. To do so will only keep me a prisoner to the past. I want to be set free. This memoir and this chapter are not a symbol of me being chained to the past but instead a way to set us all free. Freedom begins with compassion and forgiveness. Personally, I am done with anger, resentment, and negativity. Truth is not an example of negativity. The old adage that the truth will set you free is permission to release the shackles of shame, guilt, and silence. I forgive your dad for everything. Our story will change for the better when all of us learn the art of humility, kindness, and truth-telling.

Over the months, I have had to learn to forgive you, too. I was hurt and confused by your actions and your words posted within social media. But I understand. I understand more than you know. As a mother, I wanted to reach out to you and tell you that I understand your hurt, pain, and confusion. I wanted to be there for you, to support your healing, but just like your father, this is not my journey to walk. This is your journey. Only you can walk it. I am here when you are ready, but only you can walk through the desert to see what kind of a man you choose to be. As a mother, I want to see you be humble and kind.

Don't take for granted the love this life gives you
When you get where you're going
Don't forget turn back around
Help the next one in line
Always stay humble and kind.

As a toddler, you had neighborhood friends, too. Fortunately — or — unfortunately, they were girls. One was named Taylor, and you called her, "Tay-Tay." Funny, now that is the nickname given to pop-star Taylor Swift. Ms. Swift is one of the silence-breakers I mentioned in an earlier chapter. Another childhood friend was Abby. I thought you and Abby would be forever-friends, but we moved out of state and the two of you lost touch. I found it ironic that, later in life, you became romantically involved with another girl named Abby and eventually took another Abby to your senior prom. I really appreciated you inviting me to join you and the second Abby during a road race event upstate. Son, you have no idea how precious those moments spent together were to me.

Back to your childhood friend: Do you remember the group of kids from our home state? One was named Sean. He used to marvel at the fact that you had a knack for finding bugs. Children were naturally drawn to you. You were — and I am sure still are — so easy to get along with. You had a quiet, gentle soul that attracted a lot of people. You were meant to be born, son. You possess so many gifts to share with this world. I have the luxury of seeing from an outsider's perspective, looking in, what your adventures are. Thanks to the advancements within technology, such as social media, I get to watch your newest relationship blossom into something that seems quite serious. She is perfect for you. An avid outdoorsperson who can keep up with you and your adventures. I am happy for you.

I was hoping that since you have had the experience of first loves and relationships that did not pan out, that maybe now at the tender age of 22, you might understand better how some relationships begin with good intentions yet for reasons out of our control, dissolve. It is a part of being human. We humans are imperfectly perfect. I hope that you have been humble and kind as these relationships shift and change. I was also hoping that although we as individuals grow and change and fail and get back up again, you will cherish what we have had together as a mother and son. I keep wanting to tell you that I am so sorry, but truth be told, I am not sure what it is that I need to apologize for. In truth, I guess I do not need to know. I need to acknowledge your pain and validate it. And to that end, I need to state that unlike romantic relationships that ignite and fan out, a mother's love is forever. It is also unconditional. So, if I have to wait a lifetime to hold you again, to hug you again, and to whisper to you as I look into your eyes that I love you, then I will wait a lifetime.

I remember orange sherbet was your favorite dessert. You had a passion for nature and for being outdoors. I cherish the birthday parties, themed with construction trucks, trains, and toy alligators. Yes, there was a time that you were a big fan of Steve Irwin, the famed Crocodile Hunter. You loved all things that involved getting dirty and took to mountain biking as a high school student. You knew intuitively, as I did, that the best therapy for any human is to be outside in nature and to exercise. Don't forget that, son. If outsiders try to convince you that pharmaceuticals are the answer, don't fall for it. Nature. Exercise. Prayer. Mediation. Music. Arts. Connecting with others. Community. Volunteering. And truth-telling: That is when one heals. Each and every one of us will suffer at some point in our lifetimes. Our journey is individual and personal. How we heal and when we heal is up to us. So, son, as you navigate your journey, try all of the things that worked for you in the past. Those tools listed above are lifelong cures for grief and worry. You've got this, son. I have faith in you. You will get through this just fine. Keep the faith, and trust your inner voice. Follow your inner voice and your heart. Love wins, son. Lead with love, and you will never go wrong. Lastly, remember that there is one woman who has walked this Earth who loves you more than life itself, and that woman is me.

You know there's a light
That glows by the front door,
Don't forget the keys under the rug,
Childhood stars shine,
Always stay humble and kind.

Ruth Collins

Chapter 9
Life is Simple: Live Your Dream

I hope you never lose your sense of wonder,
You get your fill to eat but always keep the hunger,
May you never take one single breath for granted,
God forbid love ever leave you empty handed,
I hope you still feel small
When you stand beside the ocean,
Whenever one door closes, I hope one more opens,
Promise me that you'll give faith a fighting chance,
And when you get the choice to sit it out or dance,
I hope you dance.
~Lee Ann Womack, "I Hope You Dance"

Why the memoir you may ask? Are you trying to embarrass your family? Hurt your children?

My answer for the last two questions is, "No." It was not my life goal to write this memoir. Given that my divorce took place 12 years ago and the loss of my parental rights took place four years ago, and loss of contact with both of my children was two years ago demonstrates that writing this memoir was not my first action after my divorce. It was not until I met with several other families who have experienced some form of professional misconduct or judicial abuse that I felt compelled as well as obligated to share my story. In addition, my writing this memoir was not meant to be a retaliatory action on my part: Instead, it is a call to action for readers who have sat on the sidelines watching women and children being marginalized. I write to take away the power of those who put our family in harms ways. To harm a mother is to harm a child. To harm a child is to harm a mother. Mothers and their children are interconnected. Legal papers cannot separate our hearts. I write to empower others and to validate their experiences. I write to reunite adult children with their estranged mother. I write hoping my truths will make a difference and that the resources contained within this memoir serve as a reservoir of hope for those who suffer in silence. No, this memoir was never a childhood dream of mine.

I had other dreams. Dreams of being financially independent but not so wealthy that I forgot compassion. I had dreams of obtaining a four-year college degree and dreams of being an active participant within my children's lives. My goals and dreams for both myself and for my two children were to break the cycle of generational poverty and to end the pattern of abuse that appears to be innately handed-down from one generation to another. No. My goal was never to embarrass or hurt my family, or to damage those relationships that I hold dear to my heart. I did not ask to be targeted for maltreatment, nor did I seek out opportunities for my children to be used for another adult's gain. My dreams were shattered and so were my children's dreams. If the people who harmed us wanted me to say or write nice things about them, then maybe they should have made better choices themselves. Maybe they should have placed the wellbeing of young children ahead of professional or financial gains. My hope is that my being open about my own failures and short-comings, permits those who harmed our family to be open and honest about their short-comings and failures. If we can come together despite our differences, then maybe just maybe, the cycle of abuse will come to an end. That thought sustains my hope for our collective future as a human race.

I also write for those who no longer have their voice. Those women and children who are no longer with us. Whether it be my maternal grandmother who passed away several years ago, or the local, six-year old boy was recently murdered by his father. The young boy's name was Preston. He lived in the same state as me. I need to be his voice. I need to be his grieving mother's voice. A voice for my biological father since I have been told that he grew up in a toxic and unhealthy home environment. I need to be a voice for the children that never knew their mothers: Their relationships destroyed because of several systemic failures. No. My intent is not to hurt people or harm reputations. My intent is to speak my truths. There is great power in speaking your truth. And with that power, I hope to be a voice that inspires change. When given a choice to sit it out or dance, I have chosen to dance.

~~~~~~

Amber, this chapter is devoted to you. You were born on a Wednesday. That statement made you smile didn't it? It made you smile because I already mentioned that fact in an earlier chapter and that's what moms do, right? They repeat themselves.

Amber, one of the most amazing experiences that I remember having was seeing your big blue eyes and watching you smile at me within a day or two of your birth. There is an old adage that babies do not smile until a certain age. You clearly had a beautiful smile within 48 hours. It was then and there that I sensed something very powerful between the two of us. Like your brother Matthew, you were meant to be born. I am not repeating myself to be funny. I am stating this fact because it is true. I had no idea how much my life would change — good, bad, and ugly — because of my love for you and because of our mother-daughter bond.

First of all, it was your birth that gave me the strength to stand up to my stepfather. There was no way in hell that he was going to be in your life. I can guarantee to this day that neither you nor Matthew have any memory of him because you never met him. That was not by accident. Your birth inspired a much-needed transformation within me. I am not sure if I ever got a chance to tell you "thank you." I thank you for being the catalyst for the growth that I needed to engage in despite my fear of the work that went along with it. When you were a young child, and even as a teenager, there was never an appropriate time to explain to you why you have been a person that I look up to. Now that you are a young adult and that you have survived more challenges than I ever had to go up against, it is time to express my gratitude. Twenty-two years ago, I was very naïve and did not understand how boys have been targeted for abuse. I was brought up to believe the myth that only girls and women are targeted for sexual violence. Then the story of Adam Walsh and Jeffery Curley hit the TV news, and I was no longer naïve or ignorant. Those stories — especially the one's regarding any sexual misconduct against children — motivated me to become a child safety advocate. I started to research the topic and did whatever I could to promote positive change, not just for me as a person or for us as a family but for society-at- large. My dream was neither to become politically active nor to be vulnerable when unpacking the skeletons within our family closets. In truth telling, and in allowing myself to be vulnerable, there was empowerment. And, with empowerment, I felt I could better protect both you and your brother. This was why I was a little more over protective than either of your grandmothers. I am not judging but just acknowledging that we all thought we were doing the best we could, given our own upbringing, biases, life experiences, and education levels.

It is not until we allow ourselves to be completely vulnerable that we can truly heal and become our whole self. So, with that, I suggest that — as the song goes — when given the choice to sit it out or dance, "I hope you choose to dance."

By preschool, you demonstrated to me your love for dancing and singing. I remember taking you to preschool ballet classes. I also remember your passion for musicals. There was one day at home we watched the British version of the musical *Cats* at least four times. You were mesmerized by the dancers, costumes, and musical accompaniment. Your singing voice improved as you grew older, and it is amazing: It's a gift. I am not sure which part of the family you inherited your gift from, but it was not from me. Your father never sang either. Maybe your beautiful singing voice was something you inherited from a few generations past. My heart silently broke knowing that you never felt confident enough to pursue singing lessons or dance beyond preschool. You were very hard on yourself. Your biggest critic as a younger child was you. I think as a younger child I was also really hard on myself, but I also had a stepfather who verbally berated us whenever we upset him. So, I thought my lack of confidence was from growing up in an environment that was not very supportive. Raising both you and Matthew changed my understanding and previous judgments regarding nature versus nurture. We humans are born with an individualized chain of DNA molecules that predispose us for being who we are. Environment does play a role in character development. However, it is fascinating how in even the most supportive and loving environments, a child can exhibit anxiety and lack of confidence. I was painfully shy as a child. Sometimes the shyness was so overwhelming that I would stutter. Maybe those characteristics were inherited from my side of the family. God only knows.

As a young child and even into adulthood, you exhibited a strong love and compassion for animals. In your younger years, stuffed animals brought your great comfort. While your brother played with trains, trucks, Legos, and plastic alligators, you opted to play with stuffed animals and dress-up clothes. I remember one specific stuffed dog that was your reward for giving up your pacifier. I cannot recall his name at the moment but he — it was a "he" stuffed dog — was your comfort item at bedtime.

The funniest thing you did as a toddler was to obsess over your brother's hats. It did not matter if it was a big, floppy sun hat, a train conductor's hat, a plastic construction worker's hat, or a baseball cap. As long as it belonged to your brother, you had a knack for tracking the hat down and wearing it around the house as if it was yours. No permission. No apologies. It just was yours for the taking. That was the kind of young lady I wanted to raise. Not a lady who takes from others without asking, but a lady who does not apologize for being herself. You were under the age of two and too young to fully understand right from wrong, so your actions were not of ill intent. I believe you were expressing who you were. At that phase of your life, you were a hat-girl. You were confident those hats were meant for you. That was the confidence I was hoping you would carry into adulthood.

You did exhibit leadership skills in middle school. You had no qualms about marching down to the principal's office if you observed a classmate being bullied. I also remember you asking the middle school principal if you could place a large jug out in the lobby of the school so students could donate money toward the World Wildlife Fund. You had a mission, and that was to prevent the polar ice caps from melting in order to prevent the polar bears from becoming extinct. Your childhood was full of many, many positive memories that I hope both you and Matthew hold tight to. I tried to encourage both of you to be the person you were born to be.

Amber, you melted my heart when you typed a poem for me as a Mother's Day gift. You were in middle school at the time — probably age 13. You wrote:

Mom,

I love you Sooooo with a capital "S" much! You are the peanut to my butter...the mac to my cheese... the A-1 sauce to my steak...I don't know what I would do or where I would be without you! You helped me when I needed you, and gave advice when I was confused, sad, or lost. The best gift you gave me was a loving, caring, nurturing mom. You gave me strength when I was weak, you were my eyes when I could not see, and you gave me faith to believe. I am everything I am because you loved me. Over the years, I have noticed how you put Matthew and me first, and yourself second. You sacrificed what you wanted to make us happy, but the most amazing part, was you didn't ask for anything in return. I have tried to do that. I have tried to put myself second, and to be honest, it was a lot harder than I thought. I don't know how you do what you do. You are the best mother any child could ever ask for. I see my friend's parents who just leave their kids home alone all day while they work not caring about what their child needs or wants. I see parents who make their kids join sports and make them hang out with certain groups of kids, read certain books and follow certain dreams. Then I see you. You don't force us to be anyone we aren't. You encourage us to follow OUR hearts and to be who WE are. I could go on and on about everything that you do for us, but if it did, I would need 3 more hours to fit everything in, and the result would be a 500-page letter. So, I am going to sum this up by saying; I don't know if you realize how amazing you are. Maybe I am wrong but I think you underestimate how much of a great mother you are. So here I am telling you just in case you forget. I love you mom. You're the best. Happy Mother's Day. Love Amber.

I am so very touched by this keepsake and gift, Amber. I pray someday that we can return to the way our relationship used to be. It is so strained right now. I have no idea what kind of hell you went through when you and Matthew were court-ordered to live full-time with your father. It was a complete upheaval to all that you knew.

Our parenting styles were so different. You were just barely 12 years old. You should have been with your mother during those teenage years. Your childhood cut short. For that lost childhood, my heart will always hold compassion, empathy, and sadness. I have no answer except to say that life is far from fair. And for some reason, not one person leaves this Earth without first experiencing some form of loss, hardship, or trauma. It is not fair, but I have come to understand that it is those obstacles in life that force us to grow spiritually and as humans. If all was well and if all of our worries or concerns were instantly resolved with a snap of a finger, we would never learn to be selfless. Maybe, dear Amber, the selflessness you observed in me came from the challenging childhood that I had had. Maybe my goal of protecting you and Matthew from disappointments and injustice was a goal impossible to fulfill. For that I am deeply sorry. I am so sorry that we humans have to face some form of obstacle in life that will either destroy us or empower us to be what it is that we were born to be.

Your poem and Mother's Day gift reminds me that both you and Matthew are doing exactly what it is that I prayed that you would be able to do: I gifted you a life so that you could grow up to fulfill your dreams, not mine: to grow up to be who you were meant to be and not a shadow or miniature version of me. You were meant to be born, and it is with great excitement that I get to see who it is that you were meant to be. I just wish that we could be more communicative than we have been. I just wish we were able to see each other more than we do. Is that being selfish? Is that putting me first? If so, I hope that as I age, that I am permitted the opportunity to be a little selfish before I leave this Earth. Together, I hope we both continue to choose to dance. Amber, in the words of Lee Ann Womack, *"Don't let some hell-bent heart leave you bitter. When you come close to selling out reconsider. Give the heavens above more than just a passing glance. And when you get the choice to sit it out or dance. I hope you dance."* I hope we dance.

~~~~~~~~~~~~~~~~~~~~~

I want to share some hope with any protective mother reading this story. They say hope is eternal. I say leading with love fosters hope.

After several months of not hearing from Amber, we finally connected via text message last summer. That summer, we met for coffee the very first time in over a year. I was extremely nervous. What if Amber does not show up? What if her dad finds out and gives her the ultimatum of losing his approval and his affection if she reunites with me? What if Amber is opting to reconnect with me to demand that I never see her again? I was an emotional wreck, but at the same time, grateful for the opportunity to get some answers as to why both children became disconnected within what seemed like a matter of one week.

We met face-to-face in the summer of 2017. After we exchanged a hug, Amber presented me with a necklace that she made just for me. I was overwhelmed with joy. I had also brought gifts: one for her and one for Matthew. He did not join us. He was not ready yet, according to Amber. Our coffee date lasted about 90 minutes, and off she went to food shop. Amber was 19 at the time but presented like she was in her early twenties. Both children were forced to grow up well before their time. Both presented to the outside world as having it all together. I felt an enormous amount of pride that both children appeared to have moved forward with their lives. Amber had to take a year off from college studies to find herself. And Matthew was a full-time student entering his junior year. He had a serious girlfriend, and according to Amber, Matthew and his girlfriend were planning to travel out West soon. On the surface, all seemed well. The only information I got was the neither child wanted to discuss the past. I understood. I stated to Amber that I was just as happy to move forward and focus our time together. We agreed to stay present. We also spoke of our future goals and aspirations.

Matthew, I was left to assume, was burying his feelings and memories into a deep and dark crevasse. If he accompanied Amber, our meeting would have forced him to shed light on those memories he opted to forget about. But I knew from experience that a person can run from their past, they can bury their past, but unless you face the past and "do the work," as those in the therapy field like to say, the past has a way of rearing its ugly head at the most inconvenient time. If I could give anyone advice, it would be this: Dig deep, and face those demons as soon as possible. If you do not, you will bring those shadows and wounds into everything you do in your future, including relationships. I worry to this day that my son's inability to make peace with me will inadvertently harm any and all of his future relationships with women. I was proud of Amber for being the first one within their household to reach out and receive the proverbial olive branch from me. I have been hurt as well. I have a lot that I could be angry about, too, but I choose to let it go. It is far more fun to dance than to sit it out. To hold onto pain, hurt, anger, resentment, and pride is to become the person who never dances. I choose to dance.

~~~~~~~~~~~~~~~~~~~~~~~~

Amber and I met a few more times before the year 2018. Our time together was limited to her and myself: That was her choice, not mine. I made a conscious effort to let her lead the conversation. I let her pick the time and place we met at. I let her have choices in order to empower her again. I never said it out loud, but I completely understood that our being together was a gift from God. My prayers had been answered. No one was forcing her to speak to me. I have networked with far too many women to know that it is not uncommon for adult children to completely sever their ties with their mothers. We may never know if it is because of the lies that have been told to the children now adults, or if the trauma was far too destructive that reuniting with their mothers is too triggering. For some, forgetting and moving on as if the mother never existed seems like the easy way out of court-ordered dysfunction. I fully understood that every minute with Amber was a gift, and as such, I had to put ego aside and myself aside. No female child will ever understand the heart of a mother until they become a mother themselves. And because of this, Matthew may never fully understand the depth of my love for him or how much my heart aches from not knowing him.

If I can share one more silver lining, it is this: When I met with Amber in March of 2018, it was less than two weeks after the Valentine's Day school shooting in Florida. She wanted to discuss her feelings about the school massacre and how she felt about the student activists. She also said something that took me by surprise. She shared sentiments similar to mine, but she never knew how I felt because I never disclosed those feelings and opinions to her. She informed me that the active shooter had been adopted, and that his life prior to and after adoption was not a very good one. She explained to me how several adults and several systems failed this young man. And as a result of these failures, he turned toward violence. Her words assured me that I need not say anything anymore. I need not prove to her how much I tried to protect and support her. She understands the failures of our many systems. I took her words as an opportunity to validate her opinion that children are not born angry and violent. Neither one of us thought the active shooter's childhood was a reason to excuse his violent actions but instead thought it helped to explain his actions. If we understand the root of violence, then assuredly we can take proper action to prevent violence.

Amber's words validated what should be done to curtail violence in America. We need to dialogue about childhood trauma and how trauma unaddressed and untreated can lead to social issues later. Secretly, I said a silent prayer of thanks that my children have chosen to be nonviolent in their day-to-day actions. I was fortunate to have been their primary caregiver for the first 12 years of Amber's life and for the first 14 of Matthews's life. I think that time spent together created two resilient young adults.

Matthew is now struggling, as I understand it. He has kept his distance and has never agreed to accompany Amber when we get together. My heart continues to break for him. I have to continue to remind myself that this is his choosing: He has to choose when it is that he wants to dance. Our journeys are unique to us. Our spiritual growth happens within the perfect timing of the Universe. I can fixate on what Matthew and I do not have. Or, I can focus on what Amber and I are creating. I choose the latter. Amber and I are creating an opportunity to take back our lives: to be fully present, to be humble and kind, and, to dance. We both had our own time of sitting it out. But now, we are choosing to dance.

Amber, my heartfelt wish for you is that you always choose to dance. Keep life simple. Rid yourself of those people who complicate your life. Live your dream Amber. This is your life to live and no one else's. Live as if failure is never an option.

Tell me who wants to look back on their years
And wonder?
I hope you dance.

Ruth Collins

Chapter 10
The Future is Feminine: Be Empowered

I am unwritten, can't read my mind,
I'm undefined.
I'm just the beginning, the pen's in my hand,
Ending unplanned.
Staring at the blank page before you.
Open up the dirty window.
Let the sun illuminate the words
That you could not find.
~Natasha Bedingfield,
"Feel the Rain on Your Skin."

Natasha Bedingfield's lyrics for the above song resonate with me for so many reasons. First of all, it has two different titles when searched through Google. One source has the title listed as "Unwritten." Another source has the song listed as "Feel the Rain on Your Skin."

I love her official music video of this song, which is available on YouTube. She is strikingly beautiful, confident, and joyful and emotes empowerment within this music video. I find the lyrics within "Unwritten" to be a fitting female empowerment song for this chapter. Please take the time to watch the video if you have not done so already. I am to assume that neither title is to be considered right or wrong. They are both correct. I want to use the song title and the lyrics as metaphors for this last and final chapter. There is more than one right way to mother, live life, heal, and be empowered. Have no doubt that the future is feminine. Not female. Feminine. My advice for anyone choosing to read this memoir is to trust the process. Trust the process of life. Trust your journey. Trust your truth. Trust you. Be unwritten. Freedom is writing your story as you go through the journey of your life. Be unwritten.

I remember a conversation I had with a dear friend regarding the estrangement of my children. I had confided in him that I had intended to pen this memoir four years ago, in 2014, but I had expectations that the memoir was not specifically centered on our survival of the family court system but a sharing of a one-two-three-step process of rebuilding your life — with your children — after all the players vanished away. By players, I refer to the former husband's legal right to be enmeshed in your life post-divorce, the lawyers, the GALs, the social workers and doctors, and the well-meaning domestic abuse advocates. My vision of what was supposed to be did not happen. After being blindsided once again in July of 2015 came the crushing heartbreak, despair, and grieving process that few understood. Donna understood. Coral understood. However, the general public has no idea what grieving the loss of a child that is still living feels like.

"This was not the ending that I had envisioned writing about," I confided in my dear friend. "What if I never see or hear from my children ever again? What kind of uplifting story would that be?"

My friend responded with these words: "Write your own ending."

His words changed my idea of what one would consider a happy ending. I was intrigued. My thoughts were at odds with each other. On one hand, I wanted the memoir to be as authentic and as truthful as possible, with the only exception being the changing of the names of those I feel deserve to have their privacy protected. At the same time, I expected this memoir to be one of hope and healing — the proverbial happy ending. Our ending, at this point in time, was not one of mother-child reunification and pure bliss. I was stuck, and I am to assume the children were also stuck within a grief process that few professionals understood. Our one-two-three-step healing process clearly unwritten. We were left empty-handed, attempting to move forward with no idea how to navigate this part of our journey. Being stuck in the grief process is not the end-all of the healing process nor is it a way of life — at least not for me. "Write your own ending," my friend repeated himself.

After some thought, I thanked my friend for his out-of-the-box suggestion, and that is when I decided to stop procrastinating and start writing. My objective was not to write half-truths or to sugarcoat our experiences. However, I intentionally left out a significant amount of detail for a few important reasons — the first being parts of our truths and our story are too painful to revisit for me, and I assure you too painful for the reader as well. I did not want this memoir to be triggering for those who have suffered any form of abuse. Another reason I chose to leave out a significant amount of detail regarding the abuse is to protect my now adult children and to offer the proverbial olive branch to those who took part in our family's destruction. I have kept files of medical documents and audio court records if anyone decided to challenge me; however, I do not feel that exposing every detail of the terror we faced when navigating the family court system would actually add to the message that I wanted to convey: This memoir was meant to be about surviving, hope, taking back your voice, your power, and fostering healing. I left out the details that I felt would cloud over the message and leave the reader feeling nauseated and hopeless.

I choose to write my own ending. I choose to focus on healing. It is to be seen if my now adult son will choose to reach out to me and make efforts to resume a healthy relationship with me. This is his journey, too. I have to respect his decision and his choices. I may not agree with or like them, but because I have such deep and unconditional love for him, I know I have to let him go if I hope to get him back. This strategy — to date — seems to have worked for my daughter. I hope this reasoning resonates with you. We can choose our ending. We can choose between remaining a lifelong victim of a destructive system or becoming empowered.

In the summer of 2017, I began writing this book while simultaneously asking the Universe to provide for me the ending that I wanted. Serendipitously, it was that same summer that Amber texted me for the first time in several months. Rather than living in fear of never knowing my own children, I choose to believe that I would be reunited with them sometime in the future. I chose to lead my life as being unwritten. As Ms. Bedingfield croons, "The pen's in my hand, ending unplanned."

My friend's sage advice to write my own ending reminded me of Sophia's advice three years ago: "Petition the Universe for what you want from life. The Universe will conspire with you to achieve your dreams and goals. The challenging part is that everything happens in Divine timing and not before. So, you when you petition the Universe, you also have to let go of the outcome."

"Let go of the outcome?"

"Yes, let go of the outcome. What I mean is both parties have to be agree. It is something that the other person's soul has to agree to."

Sophia would, on occasion, lose me. In other words, I did not always understand what she meant. Over time and with practice, I was beginning to understand faith to be more spiritual than religious. Her idea of faith was very different than the faith lessons I had been raised with. How I was beginning to understand faith is that life is not about good things only happening to good people. Prayer and petitions were not as simple as "ask and you shall receive." No faith is not that simple. Faith is trusting that your Higher Power is with you at all times. Patience is a part of faith as you are in commune with that Higher Power. Together, you and your Higher Power will create miracles. The impossible soon becomes possible. I have witnessed this over and over again. Since I have opened my mind, my heart, and my eyes, I have witnessed the power of faith over and over again. The foundation of those witnessed miracles is love, faith, patience, and truly letting go of expectations. I found that once I learned to let go of any and all expectations, everything that was once chaotic became peaceful. Everything that I had lost — my home, my savings, my autonomy and independence, my joyful spirit — was returning to me, piece by piece. I assure you that there is truly a light at the end of what appears to be a very long and dark tunnel.

~~~~~~~~~~~~~~~~~~~~~~~~~~~~

Reaching for something in the distance,
So close you can almost taste it,
Release your innovations—
Feel the rain on your skin.
No one else can feel it for you.
Only you can let it in.
No one else, no one else

Can speak the words on your lips.

If I can offer any advice for promoting healing, it is this: Allow yourself to feel things. Feel your emotions. Feel the rain on your skin. Name the feeling; confront it, and embrace the feeling. Name the feeling; confront it, and then dismiss that feeling by letting it float away towards the sky if it is a feeling that does not lift you up to being your best self. Feel it, then release it. Humans feel. Healthy humans allow themselves to feel their feelings. It is unhealthy to shove feelings deep down into your soul. Filing your feelings down into the lowest resources of your being is as toxic and unhealthy as keeping secrets that are not meant to be kept. Secrets entangled with shame, fear, or guilt are manifesting negative emotions and energies that will not serve you. Suppressing and denying your right to feel your feelings will not serve you either. In order to grow into your best self, you need to release your inhibitions and become empowered.

~~~~~~~~~~~~~~~~~~~~~~

Our future is, without a doubt, feminine. Please let me explain. About five years ago, my daughter Amber sent me a picture text message of some new age books that she thought would be of interest to me. I was somewhat perplexed because, at that time, I would not have characterized myself as spiritual. Within Amber's cell phone picture was the book, "Spontaneous Evolution." Living in separate homes and having little face-to-face contact with her, I desperately wanted to connect with her. So, upon her recommendation, I bought the audio-book. I figured if we read the same book, it would give us something positive to focus on when we spoke next.

At that time, I had a three-hour roundtrip commute to work each day. I felt listening to the audio-book during my commute would be a good use of my time. Written on the cover of the box that contained the five CDs were the words, "Our positive future and how to get there from here," as well as, "Our golden opportunity to write the next chapter in human evolution." The science contained within the CDs was intriguing. I was completely enchanted by the author and biologist Bruce H. Lipton and political and cultural commentator Steve Bhaerman. At first, their predictions of our collective future were difficult to wrap my head around, but over time, it all started to make sense. Their book gave me hope. In a very scientific way, their book gave the answer to the age-long and controversial question, "What is the meaning of life?" When the authors stated that our world was headed for chaos and a dismantling of systems that had been established for centuries, well, I envisioned a time a hundred years from now. The authors insisted that in order for humanity to evolve, this time of chaos needed to take place within the next few decades. Time was of the essence. Impossible, I thought. Even though, on a personal level, I had gone through the process of losing everything I had as possessions and everything that I had as a sense of security, such as faith communities and the court process, I still did not understand that our world as we knew it was also going through a rebirth. Soon after listening to this audio-book, I discovered that I was not the only person experiencing significant loss. And the systems in our world that we had faith in were being exposed for their failures.

I have come to understand that individual, as well as collective, losses are meant to create a stronger, braver, and more empowered individual and humanity, as well as a more humane, peaceful, and enlightened world. Unfortunately, the process is extremely difficult and painful. Our present world — in my opinion — is in a complete tailspin because, up until now, our moral compass and, our values as a society and as a race have been, more often than not, exclusively ruled with a masculine energy. In my experience, masculine energy is often an energy compelled to overpower; an energy that uses intimidation, fear, force, and weaponry to get one's needs met. For me, it is the opposite of feminine energy. Feminine energy gives life and respects life. It is brave. Feminine energy nurtures, promotes peace, and respects all of humanity and Mother Earth. Feminine energy is founded in love, while masculine energy is founded in fear. Feminine energy asks the questions, "How can I help you, and how can I support life?" Masculine energy is more concerned with ego, and winning. I believe that all humans possess characteristics that are both feminine and masculine. This is not a gender issue but a moral compass and character issue. Leaders who possess feminine energy are leaders who lead with heart and mind: We do not separate the mind from the body. The masculine energy that has ruled our Earth to date has led with the mind separated from the heart.

My point in sharing my opinions with you is to assure you that we are not facing the end of the world. Instead, as stated within *The Book of Joy* and *Spontaneous Evolution*, we are shifting — evolving — toward a more humane humanity: The future is feminine and welcomes male warriors to rise up with us and work toward peace. A loving and peaceful society will not condone violence as a way of life. The national March For Our Lives movement is a perfect example. The march took place on March 24, 2018 — barely a month after the February 14th high school massacre in Florida, these teenage activists organized a movement that has our political leaders are paying attention. The teenagers responding to the school shootings that took place at Parkland High School are both males and females. Together, they have chosen to speak truth to power. I happened to catch a few minutes of the televised CNN media coverage as one of the teenagers spoke. She spoke of how she and others like her were "thrown into activism." She added, "We march. We fight. We roar." Her statements made me smile and brought me hope for our future. Her statements reminded me of the warriors within the protective mothers' movement. We, too, marched during The Women's March in 2017 and 2018. We, too, were thrown into activism. We, too, know what it is like to be characterized as angry, irrational, and other adjectives meant to question your own truths.

My advice is to dig deep and to come out even stronger and louder. Remember, as I mentioned in an earlier chapter, when an activist speaks truth to power, the first thing the opposition will do is dismiss you and attack your character and credibility. It is their go-to move: Embrace it. It means you are being an effective agent for change. Change scares most people. Remember to operate from a standpoint of love and not fear. As the saying goes, be the change you want to see.

When groups of people are thrown into activism, they do not do so from a standpoint of being reactionary. These people are mobilized from a standpoint of feeling compelled to offer life-sustaining options — alternatives — for our day-to-day existence. We want to improve our world. It is not a self-serving movement: It is self-preserving movement. Self-preserving as a collective, not as an individual. The Florida teenage activists are our future. They are not self-righteous or arrogant. They are selfless, articulate, intelligent, and empowered.

Watching television coverage of the national march, I thought, "This is it." This is what Bruce H. Lipton and Steve Bhaerman referenced. Rather than fearing out futures, I feel hope. Despite what has happened to me and my children, I have hope. Our stories are not over yet. Together, we activists and warriors will build bridges, not walls. And with those bridges we will unite in our differences and create the world that was meant to be.

Drench yourself in words unspoken.
Live your Life with arms wide open.
Today is where your book begins.
The rest is still unwritten…

How does one heal from trauma? The answer to that question is not the same for everyone. I am not a doctor or a lawyer. I cannot provide for you their professional advice. This portion of the memoir is not meant to be the be-all, end-all recipe for healing. However, it is a list of tools, as I like to call them that worked at different times along my journey. Some I had to really learn to be open to. Those were the healing tools that probably helped me the most, the ones that broke down everything I had ever known and forced me to be open to something I never thought I would be open to — such as the metaphysical healing power of crystals and essential oils.

For me, the thought process of being open to new ideas and actions was the opposite of insanity. Remember the old saying? "What do you call doing something over, and over, and over again while expecting a different outcome?" The answer, as we all know, is insanity. It was clear to me that since my old way of thinking and my old way of problem-solving was not working for me anymore, I had to be open to other tools for healing. If my goal was to find joy again and to grow to be my best version of me, I had to be open to other options—options that at first felt foreign to me but over time made sense and felt ideal for me. I will list these tools as bullet-points as I do not want to create a bias for you on which tools I found was most effective and important. For those readers seeking to heal past traumas, I remind you that this is your journey. Your life is your story: You write your ending. You decide which tool or combination of tools will promote your sense of healing.

- Limit screen time and get outside: Nature is an amazing healer!
- Exercise: yoga, running, surfing, walking, biking
- Music
- Mediation, prayer, and faith practices
- Healing crystals such as Selenite, Hematite, and Tourmaline
- Essential oils: doTerra has a set of oils specific for emotional healing.
- Sing, dance, play an instrument
- Creative endeavors: Write your story; take an art class; make jewelry.
- Find support: Build your support system through reliable sources.
- Talk therapy: Find someone who has specialized training in trauma and grief counselling.
- Quiet time: When you become comfortable with silence, you find your answers.
- Practice self-care daily
- Good nutrition and healthy beverages: Treat your body with respect!
- Therapeutic massage
- Volunteer and engage in activism: Be sure to fill your own well first, however.
- Rid yourself of all toxic people and environments.
- Surround yourself with positive books, people, and movies.
- Engage in random acts of kindness.
- Write messages in the sand if you are close to a beach.

In closing, I want to state that it is not lost on me that the completion of this memoir — in its most humble form — is nearly one year to the date after the Easter weekend in which I was able to speak with my daughter for the first time since the summer of 2016. It is also not lost on me that the catalyst for me being a child-safety advocate was the Columbine school shooting. I do not find it a coincidence that it is the weekend of The March for Our Lives event that I find myself ready to end this memoir with the ending now written. It is not a coincidence that 2018 is the year of the silence-breakers and, the #metoo and #timesup movements. None of this is lost on me. As my friend Sophia taught me, everything happens in Divine timing and not before.

I had planned to write this memoir a few years back, but I never did. My creative thought was the BRAVE tattoo positioned on my left shoulder was the perfect book cover and *Brave* would be the name given to the memoir. However, Rose McGowan recently published her memoir by the same title. Clearly, the title was meant for her and not me. *Writings in the Sand* was the brilliant recommendation given to me by my editor. I found her idea to be absolutely perfect given the amount of healing I derived from walking to and from the beach. The beach became my opportunity to communicate to my children by writing in the sand. You could say it was there, at the beach, that I sought my Higher Power's support in creating the proper ending to my story — not the perfect ending but the proper one. What happens next is unwritten.

RESOURCES

BOOKS

Nothing But My Voice, written by Donna Buiso. Author can be followed on Facebook.

The Quincy Solution: Stop Domestic Violence and Save $500 Billion, written by Barry Goldstein, http://stopabusecampaign.com.

Persecuted But Not Silenced, written by Maralee McLean. Authors' website: maraleemclean.com

The Worse Interests of the Child, written by Keith Harmon Snow.

Women on Trial, written by Phyllis Chesler.

Coercive Control: How Men Entrap Women in Personal Life, written by Evan Stark.

The Boy Who Was Raised as a Dog, written by Dr. Bruce Perry.

The Batterer as a Parent, authored by Lundy Bancroft, Jay Silverman, and Daniel Ritchie.

How We Love Our Kids, co-authored by Milan and Kay Yerkovich.

The Beast I Loved: A Battered Woman's Desperate Struggle To Survive released from WildBlue Press on March 13, 2018, and written by Robert Davidson.

Motherless America, and, *Trumpian Abuse:Government & Family Systems that Prop-Up the Male Regime*, written by Doreen Ludwig. Authors' website: maccabuse.org

Don't Hug Your Mother, a memoir written by Gareth and Fintan Murphy. Authors' website donthugyourmother.com

Hanging On By My Fingernails: Surviving the New Divorce Gamesmanship, and How a Scratch Can Land You in Jail, written by Janie Mc Queen.

F.I.F.I: Finical Infidelity F**K IT, written by Jodi Parmley. Authors' website: www.jodiparmley.com

Beyond the Hostage Child: Towards Empowering Protective Parents, written by Leorna N. Rosen, Ph.D.

Why Does He Do That? Inside the Minds of Controlling Men, and, *The Batterer as a Parent*, written by Lundy Bancroft. Authors' website: lundybancroft.com

Mother Erased: Learning, Leaving & Losing My Children to a Sociopath, written by Christine Ackerlund.

Epidemic: America's Trade in Child Rape, written by Dr. Lori Handrahan.

Without Conscience: The Disturbing World of the Psychopaths Among Us, written by Robert D. Hare, PhD.

The Sociopath Next Door, written by Martha Stout.

Women Who Love Psychopaths: Inside the Relationships of inevitable arm With Psychopaths, Sociopaths & Narcissists, written by Sandra L. Brown, MA.

FILMS

Resilience: https://educate.tugg.com/titles/resilience

Paper Tigers: https://educate.tugg.com/titles/paper-tigers

Bundle: https://educate.tugg.com/titles/paper-tigers-resilience-bundle

Family Court Crisis- Our Children at Risk, The Center for Judicial Excellence.

What Doesn't Kill Me, produced by Rachel Meyrick: www.whatdoesntkillme.com

WEBSITES

http://acestoohigh.com/ Adverse Childhood Experiences (ACE).

www.domesticviolenceexpert.org ~Julie Owens: Violence Against Women Consultant.

www.domesticshelters.org/domestic.violence.books/child_custo dy

centerforjudicalexcellence.org ~ The Center for Judicial Excellence.

caprotectiveparents.org ~ California Protective Parents Association.

nurturedparent.org ~ The Nurtured Parent.

www.crpcwatch.org ~ The Center for the Rights and Protection of Children.

coralanikatheill.comCoral Anika Theill: author, advocate, speaker & reporter.

tinaswithin.com Tina Swithin, LLC: author, coach and advocate.

HEALING

Monochrome Days: A First-Hand Account of One Teenager's Experience With Depression, written by Cait Irwin, along with Dwight L. Evans, M.D., and Linda Wasmer Andews.

Energy Medicine with Donna Eden. Website: www.innersource.net/em

"*The Trauma Project*," Facebook page.

Journaling into Perspective: A gentle guide for bringing life priorities into focus, written by Leslie Orr.

Belleruth Naparstek "*Guided Imagery for Trauma Recovery.*" Websites: wellbaskets.com and healthjourneys.com

Option B: Facing Adversity, Building Resilience, and Finding Joy, written by Sheryl Sandberg and Adam Grant. Website: optionb.org

Searching for Angela Shelton documentary, and, *Finding Angela Shelton*, book. Website: www.angelashelton.com

Author Brene Brown's TED Talk video, "*The Power of Vulnerability.*"

Be Your Own Hero Warrior Workbook: for survivors, warriors, advocates, loved ones, and supporters ready to move past pain and suffering and reclaim joy and happiness, written by Angela Shelton.

The Book of Joy: Lasting Happiness in a Changing World, written by Dalai Lama and Desmund Tutu.

Peaceful Mind Peaceful Life, Facebook page.

Tiny Buddha, Facebook page.

Divine Feminine Reawakening, Facebook page.

How We Love, co-authors Milan & Kay Yerkovich. Website: howwelove.com

Abraham Hicks 2018, new meditations, found within website: serenitytalk.com

The Crystal Bible: A Definitive Guide to Crystals, written by Judy Hall.

EPILOGUE

April 21, 2018

Dear Investigative Reporter,

I am a mother living near Boston. I wish to have the opportunity to share my horrific experience going through a recent divorce in the Essex County family court system. I filed for divorce in December 2011. It was final in March 2015. During the course of that time, my ex-husband isolated our teenaged daughter from me by means of coercive control. He continues to subject her to severe psychological abuse. I will give a brief overview.

Over the last 15 years, the behavior of my then-husband became more abusive, and sexually inappropriate. Both my daughter and I reported his abuse and strange behavior to therapists, doctors, teachers, school nurses, as well as friends, family and neighbors. He was reported to DCF several times. I had hoped that the three therapists involved with us would help us, but two of them colluded with my ex-husband. In 2011, my then-fourteen-year-old daughter reported to high school staff about her father's increasingly threatening and sexually inappropriate behavior. They called police. A domestic violence officer and detective arrived at the school and interviewed my daughter and myself. Police pressed me to get my husband out of the home to protect my daughter. I filed for divorce a few months later.

Upon filing for divorce, I suddenly found myself in a series of disturbing family court events that seemed to forever be beyond my control. My daughter was quickly secreted away from me by my ex-husband with the aid of two of those therapists. I have seen little of my daughter since. My husband quickly brought in a Guardian ad Litum who was supposed to give a recommendation on custody. At the time, I did not know that this was an unusual step so early in a divorce. I requested that the GAL have experience with sexual abuse cases. To the GAL, I related my husband's strange and abusive behavior. I gave the GAL copies of the police report and DCF reports but she was not interested in them. Time after time, the GAL dismissed my words. During one of these meetings, the GAL became physically aggressive toward me.

As the months dragged on, I repeatedly tried to contact my daughter but got no response. She became unable to function in school and was put in special programming. She had previously been a very good student. While living with her father and isolated from me, she was put on anti-depressants and anti-anxiety medications. She had never been on medication before. None of this seemed to matter to the GAL.

More court personnel were brought in adding to the increasingly high cost of the divorce. I was manipulated into agreeing to have my daughter sent to a boarding school. My daughter ended up first in a therapeutic camp and then a so-called therapeutic boarding school far away. She was there for over a year and staff would not allow me to see or talk to her contrary to what I had been told would happen. Shortly after my daughter left the boarding school, it suddenly shut down with multiple reports of abuse of the students. During this time and ongoing, I have had very little, to no contact with my daughter.

Up until I filed for divorce, I had a close and loving relationship with my daughter. I was married to someone who is very abusive to both myself and my daughter. He was sexually inappropriate with her. Aided by court personnel and two of the therapists who were aligned with him, my ex-husband succeeded in isolating our daughter from me. She is his hostage. I think about her and worry about her daily. She continues to be on psychiatric medications. I don't know what will happen to her.

I understand that you are interested in writing for publication about the family courts. Please tell me how to proceed in relating these events in more detail as I hope to help expose the corruption in the family courts.

Thank you for reading this.

Regards,

Alice Louise Sheraton, Massachusetts resident

NO LOVE DEEPER

Written by Lundy Bancroft and reprinted with his permission:

There is no love deeper, more complete, and more vulnerable than the love that caring parents feel for their children. There is a bond so strong that it can be hard to tell exactly where the parent ends and the child begins, and the line is even harder to draw when our children are very young. Mothers have an additional bond from having carried their children inside of their bodies and having given birth to them, and more than half of mothers have experienced a deepened attachment through breast-feeding their babies. And mothers are, in the great majority of cases, their children's primary caretakers, especially during their early years. All connections between caring, non-abusive parents and their children are so important as to be almost sacred, but there is usually a particular quality to the mother-child bond. That life-giving and sustaining connection deserves the full support and admiration of communities and nations.

And just as there is a special beauty and importance to relationships between mothers and their children, there is a special and extraordinary cruelty in the abusive man who attempts to break or weaken the mother-child bond, whether by turning children against their mother, by harming the children physically, sexually or psychologically, or by attempting to take custody of the children away from her.

Children need protection from their abusive parents. In the realm of custody litigation which involves abuse, the abusive parent tends to be the father while the protective parent is usually the mother, because most perpetrators of domestic violence and of child sexual abuse are male. We don't know that much about what happens to protective fathers, since their cases are much less common, but we know that protective mothers frequently encounter a system that is insensitive, ignorant about the dynamics of abuse, and biased against women. In this context, mothers sometimes find themselves being forbidden by the court from protecting their children from a violent, cruel, or sexually abusive father. And this outcome is a tragic one, for children and for their mothers.

On behalf of the hundreds of people across the continent who are currently working for family court justice, I want to communicate to you our caring and solidarity with the challenging road you have ahead of you, as you fight to keep your children safe in body and soul. I want to let you know how critically important we believe that project to be, and how much your children need you to stand up for their rights and their well-being. You deserve admiration, not criticism, for the courageous risks you are taking on their behalf, and for your determination that all of you should have the opportunity to live in freedom and kindness.

Our society is currently giving mothers a powerful and crazy-making mixed message. First, it says to mothers, "If your children's father is violent or abusive to you or to your children, you should leave him in order to keep your children from being exposed to his behavior." But then, if the mother does leave, the society many times appears to do an abrupt about-face, and say, "Now that you are spilt up from your abusive partner, you must expose your children to him. Only now you must send them alone with him, without you even being around anymore to keep an eye on whether they are okay." What do we want? Do we want mothers to protect their children from abusers, or don't we?

The sad result of this double-bind is that many mothers who take entirely appropriate steps to protect their children from exposure to abuse are being insulted by court personnel, harshly and unethically criticized and ridiculed in custody evaluations and psychological assessments, and required to send their children into unsupervised contact or even custody with their abusive fathers. And sometimes these rulings are coming in the face of overwhelming evidence that the children have both witnessed abuse and suffered it directly, evidence that would convince any reasonable and unbiased person that the children were in urgent need of protection. Family courts across the US and Canada appear to be guilty day in and day out of reckless endangerment of children.

Fortunately, there are also many women who do succeed in keeping their children safe post-separation. Some manage to persuade judges to grant the mother appropriate right to keep her children safe. Others lost in the early stages but do better later, as the abuser finally starts to show his true colors over time. Some women find that they succeed best by staying out of court, and using other methods to protect their children, such as waiting for the abuser to lose interest and drop out, or moving some distance away so that he will tire. Some women find that what works best is to focus on involving their children in supportive services, connecting them to healthy relatives, and teaching them to think critically and independently, so that they become strong children who see through the abuse and manipulation.

There is no formula that works for everyone. What strategies will work best for you depends on what your local court system is like, how much support you are receiving from friends and relatives, how much internal strength your children have, and how much (or how little) damage the abuser has already succeeded in doing to your relationships with your children. And each abuser is different. Some, for example, can be placated if they feel like they have won, and will gradually drift off, while others will never be satisfied with anything less than completely alienating children from their mother. Lawyers can advise you on court strategy, therapists can share their insight into children's injuries and healing processes, but ultimately you have to rely most on your own judgment, because you are the only expert on the full complexities of your specific situation.

As you make your way ahead, I hope you will put a high priority on taking good care of yourself. Seek out kind, supportive people who are good listeners. Nurture your friendships and family relationships. Try to step through the stress long enough each day to spend some time showering your children with love if they are with you, and make sure to play with them, not just look after their needs. Notice what you have already done well, as a parent and as an advocate for your children. Give yourself credit for your own strength, and celebrate the fact that your mind is getting free of the abuse, even if your children are not free yet. Cry out your sorrows when you need to, sob into a pillow behind a closed door so you won't upset your children, but do sob, because your heart needs the cleansing relief of those tears. And then build on your strengths and accomplishments to keep fighting.

I wish the "justice system" dispensed justice, but where it comes to child custody litigation involving abusive fathers, outcomes are mixed at best. With adequate knowledge and planning, and especially if you are among the fortunate mothers who are able to obtain competent legal representation from a lawyer who understands what abusers are like as parents, you may be able to keep your children on the path to healing. If your case goes poorly, there are still ways that you can help your children feel your love and support surrounding them, and give them the strength to survive their father's destructiveness. But regardless of the outcome you experience personally, you might want to keep the following points in mind:

a. The custody system in the US and Canada is broken. You are not the only person who has experienced unhealthy and biased responses, and you are not the crazy, paranoid, vindictive person they may be painting you as.

b. Other women need your help to change that system, so that protective mothers start receiving proper respects for their rights and their children's rights.

Depending on where your own case stands currently, you may have trouble imagining any involvements right now beyond your day-to-day survival, and your efforts to keep your children functioning. But involvement in social change efforts is not necessarily separate from personal healing. Many women have found that when they become active in the protective parents' movement, raising their voices loudly for the custody rights of mothers who have been battered or whose children have been sexually abused, their own healing leaps forward. Breaking down personal isolation sometimes goes hand in hand with breaking down political isolation. So I offer suggestions here not only for ways to carry on your own fight, but also for avenues to join forces with other women (and male allies) who are working for social justice, so that protective mothers and their children can stop being torn apart.

I want to express my personal gratitude to you for your efforts to protect your children from abuse, and to raise them into caring, kind, humane values. The whole world benefits when you fight for your children's rights, and for their freedom. Protective mothers are some of our society's most invisible and most important heroes, even while they are treated so often, in a bitter irony, as villains."

~~~~~~~~~~~~~~~~~~~~~~

END CURRENT, SYSTEMIC, AND ONGOING HUMAN RIGHTS VIOLATIONS
IN FAMILY COURT

Reprinted with permission from the Minnesota Coalition for Family Court Reform, 2018.

If so moved, please share Writings in the Sand *as well as these action steps with your local legislators. Safe homes lead to safe schools, which lead to safe communities; our nation's children deserve nothing less.*

1)   Create a system of judicial accountability. Are judges following state laws? Absolute power corrupts absolutely. Self-regulation is an especially bad idea when it comes to the judiciary.

2)   Punish perjury. Routinely and without exception.

3)   Ban the Association of Family and Conciliation Courts (AFCC), a trade organization training family court professionals in discredited theories and practices that cause childhood trauma and hide evidence of abuse.

4)   Update the definition of domestic violence (coercive control). Emotional abuse has a significant and lasting effect, including physical harm. DV is not a gender-neutral issue. National and international research and statistics demonstrate that domestic violence affects 90% females; 10% males. Expertise regarding DV and DV by Proxy must be immediately and routinely utilized to protect battered women and children from contact with abusers. Restraining orders and orders for protection apply in court as well as outside of court. End "Friendly Parent" expectations and parenting class education for victims of domestic violence trying to leave with children via family court.

5)   Child abuse and domestic abuse are not caused by mental illness. Why are we relying exclusively on forensic psychiatric evaluations in cases of contested child custody?

6)   Create a Primary Caregiver Doctrine related to ACE study findings-Transferring care of children from primary caregiver after divorce increases childhood trauma.<<Removing a child from a primary caregiver for even short periods of time can have detrimental developmental consequences that may

persist well into adolescence and adulthood.>>http://bit.ly/2xkBbYS Chief Justice Neely of the West Virginia Supreme Court of Appeals on the implications of reliance on judicial discretion related to "Best Interests" criteria in contested child custody cases: "I cannot imagine an issue more subject to personal bias than a decision about which parent is 'better.' The decision may hinge on the judge's memory of his or her own parents or on his or her distrust of an expert whose eyes are averted once too often." Contrary to popular misconceptions, children do not need both parents equally. They need their primary attachment figure more than the other parent and they need the safe parent more than an abusive one.

7)   Revoke ALL gender-targeted funding related to child custody determinations. Deciding child custody based on gender alone is dangerous for children. State courts are tempted to ignore evidence of child abuse in order to garner substantial federal funding Appendix B pp. 23-29 http://bit.ly/2gL5Z9d

8)   Create eligibility requirements in federal guidelines to the states regarding child custody determinations. Without eligibility requirements, states will continue to have an incentive to limit children's involvement with an otherwise willing, caring, loving, and fit parent. The *state* is the welfare recipient http://bit.ly/2imeTgT.

9)   Ratify the ERA and CEDAW. Women must be legally defined as "people" in the United States in order to legally protect their children.

ABOUT THE AUTHOR

Ruth Collins lives with her supportive husband and family cat. Ruth and Joseph take turns reaching out to Amber and Matthew, hoping to build a bridge toward becoming a family once again. In the meantime, they spend their leisure time volunteering and traveling the world. It is their hope that this memoir becomes a healing agent for those who have suffered from any form of trauma or abuse. Ruth firmly believes that in our collective storytelling, our souls begin to heal. Her newest motto — inspired by Maya Angelou — is, "After you heal, go out and support another person's healing. Collectively, we have the power to heal not only ourselves but also our world."

Ruth Collins

Starry Night Publishing

Everyone has a story...

Don't spend your life trying to get published! Don't tolerate rejection! Don't do all the work and allow the publishing companies reap the rewards!

Millions of independent authors like you, are making money, publishing their stories now. Our technological know-how will take the headaches out of getting published. Let "Starry Night Publishing.Com" take care of the hard parts, so you can focus on writing. You simply send us your Word Document and we do the rest. It really is that simple!

The big companies want to publish only "celebrity authors," not the average book-writer. It's almost impossible for first-time authors to get published today. This has led many authors to go the self-publishing route. Until recently, this was considered "vanity-publishing." You spent large sums of your money, to get twenty copies of your book, to give to relatives at Christmas, just so you could see your name on the cover. Now, however, the self-publishing industry allows authors to get published in a timely fashion, retain the rights to your work, keeping up to ninety-percent of your royalties, instead of the traditional five-percent.

We've opened up the gates, allowing you inside the world of publishing. While others charge you as much as fifteen-thousand dollars for a publishing package, we charge less than five-hundred dollars to cover copyright, ISBN, and distribution costs. Do you really want to spend all your time formatting, converting, designing a cover, and then promoting your book, because no one else will?

Our editors are professionals, able to create a top-notch book that you will be proud of. Becoming a published author is supposed to be fun, not a hassle.

At Starry Night Publishing, you submit your work, we create a professional-looking cover, a table of contents, compile your text and images into the appropriate format, convert your files for eReaders, take care of copyright information, assign an ISBN, allow you to keep one-hundred-percent of your rights, distribute your story worldwide on Amazon, Barnes & Noble and many other retailers, and write you a check for your royalties. There are no other hidden fees involved! You don't pay extra for a cover, or to keep your book in print. We promise! Everything is included! You even get a free copy of your book and unlimited half-price copies.

In four short years, we've published more than fifteen-hundred books, compared to the major publishing houses which only add an average of six new titles per year. We will publish your fiction, or non-fiction books about anything, and look forward to reading your stories and sharing them with the world.

We sincerely hope that you will join the growing Starry Night Publishing family, become a published author and gain the world-wide exposure that you deserve. You deserve to succeed. Success comes to those who make opportunities happen, not those who wait for opportunities to happen. You just have to try. Thanks for joining us on our journey.

www.starrynightpublishing.com

www.facebook.com/starrynightpublishing/

Made in the USA
Middletown, DE
17 May 2018